© Eleanor Jolliffe 2015

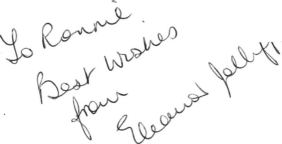

ALL RIGHTS RESERVED to: Eleanor Jolliffe

No reproduction of any text by written mechanical or

electronic means without the written permission of the

author.

ISBN-13: 978-1523334094

Create Space Independent Publishing.

This book is dedicated to the memory of my inspirational parents who travelled the world, brought back interesting objects and talked about their travels.

They circled the world three times, visited places now too dangerous to visit, and never lost their interest in travel, and did everything to encourage me. Cavorting was a favourite word of my Dad's to describe anything to do with going somewhere whether on a Clyde Steamer, or Ferry or going by ship to the Isle of Man.

Their great love was travelling by ship and my Dad was an avid collector of all things to do with shipping especially about White Star and Cunard, as he grew up on the Clyde and saw the great ships being built.

Index.

Chapter1.

Adventures start in strange ways!

My travels started when a friend of many years, asked
me to accompany her to Portugal to visit friends she had
made when living there. My first passport was applied
for and obtained, at this point several of my sons' friends
were amazed that I didn't already have one, also found it
hilarious as they already were travelling everywhere
outside UK with their parents. As my mother got her first
passport at 57 when she was ten years older than I was
at that time, I thought I was ahead on points. My travel at
that point had been going camping holidays with our
family when they were young, and going as far as Devon
and Cornwall!

In February 1993 we got the train to Manchester and
eventually found our way to the airport in a taxi with
another couple who also had stood at a bus stop waiting

in vain for a bus saying it was going to Manchester Airport.

We were flying with TAP the national Portuguese airline, and it was exciting as it was my first flight. I thoroughly enjoyed it, although when I squeaked as it was a steep take-off, (an airbus was taking off under us to go to Islamabad at a lower angle), my friend remarked to the whole plane, well those that could hear, ITS HER FIRST FLIGHT! It was like being on the waltzer at the fairground! That was the start of my love affair with travel. On arriving at Lisbon I was fortunate that my friend had warned me there would be armed soldiers, as otherwise I would have been rather surprised. Her friend who lived in Portugal was meeting us as we were going to stay with her and her husband. We had a wonderful week staying in a small town behind Caiscais. They took us to a restaurant one evening where the food was served to you on a hot stone so it cooked to your own taste, it was brilliant.

5

We went into Lisbon one day on the train and dealt with the business which was the reason for the trip, then we wandered about and I had the sights explained to me. Loved the Monument of the Discoveries, St Jeronimos Monastery, where we saw the most beautiful Arum Lilies growing, the Tile museum, and even just walking down Avenida du Liberdad was an experience. I had been warned too that hawkers would try to catch our eye and sell us tablecloths etc. One guy tried and said his wife had been up all night making the table cloth, which was a hoot, as it was made in Madeira, so she would have been hard pushed to get it onto the street in Lisbon the next day.

After having a good wander around we then caught the train to Estoril and walked from there back to Caiscais along a lovely promenade, carrying our jackets as although February it was warm. We walked past where the famous Casino is but just looked, fortunately it was closed.

6

One day they took us to Boca Inferno where the sea pounds in spectacularly, it was worth seeing, and well named.

Another day we went to Sintra which was a most interesting town and climbed the hill to get to the Palaces, we also found a little café which was totally dedicated to Formula 1 racing and featured the national racing hero. Photographs of Ferraris everywhere and everything was red and white. After we had some lunch we continued our sight- seeing and found a shop selling leather goods, and I bought myself a lovely suede coat, which I am glad to say I still have 22 years later and can still wear!

Towards the end of the week, we were taken to an out of town shopping mall which at that time was the largest in Europe, it was called Caiscais Shopping. It was an amazing place, with several levels, and the costumes from the Mardi Gras in Rio de Janeiro were on display along all the Malls, they were stunning! The colours and ostrich feathers were quite a sight, the height of the headdresses were spectacular.

A very interesting outing one of the days was to Carcavelos Market, a street market, where they sold terracotta dishes and casseroles, real traditional Portuguese table ware. Needless to say, I had to buy some to bring home, as a chicken cooked in one of these is really good. They also had the prettiest towels with applique flowers on them, so of course I was tempted and gave in and bought some to bring home.

We went to the Church of Scotland on the Sunday which is St. Andrew's which was the same name as the church I attended at home. After the service we adjourned downstairs and outside if desired as the sun was shining. I was amazed that we were offered wine not just tea or coffee like at home, a very hospitable and pleasant way to meet after the service.

All too soon, we had to head home, and on leaving we were invited to pick oranges and lemons from the trees in the garden to take home, the freshest fruit we had ever eaten.

Portugal revisited

However I was so inspired by this trip that a couple of years later I got the chance to go again, and went with a friend from North of England who was up for a jaunt. We flew to Heathrow and met up there, then caught a flight to Lisbon where we stayed in the Novotel Hotel in Lisbon. It had been a deal with Victoria Wine shops if you bought three bottles of Vinho Verde there was a holiday offer three days for the price of two with the option to add on an extra day or two at £12 per day. I fortunately had taken in all I had been shown, and had great fun showing   Val all the sights and even managed to take her to the church where we met the friends I had stayed with on the first trip, who immediately swept us up and took us to their house for a little while, before returning us to Caiscais to get a train back to Lisbon. It was a four day trip that time, but we saw lots sampled the local wines, and even got complimentary drinks from the bar as we had tried to speak some Portuguese. We found a lovely little café outside one day near St. Georges Castle and had Caldo Verde their cabbage soup it was delicious, again it was February and we could sit outside. We enjoyed visiting St Georges castle and the Tile Museum was amazing with the variety of tiles on display, but got caught out at the Monument of the Discoveries, as this very friendly man offered to tell us about all the figures, now he was speaking in Portuguese and I was at that time learning it having been inspired by my previous visit, and was following what he said. The fact he was actually tossing out famous names, we knew who he was talking about. Crunch time came when we went to bid farewell, and his hand came out palm up, talk about cross my palm with silver? It was so obvious, and as two foreigners, we were not about to cause any stir or ourselves any bother, so the palm was suitably adorned with some coins. At this time it was still the Escudos. We think we got off lightly, but another lesson was learned. Firstly as previous visit no eye contact, secondly if eye contact made and a description of something historic starts, turn back and walk away. Obviously I didn't follow the first rule to have been caught out.

Chapter 2

Canada

My next trip was to Canada, to visit my husband's elderly Aunt and his cousins, who had visited us on more than one occasion. This was really exciting as going a six hour flight was an adventure, and travelling alone. I was eventually met at Pearson International by an old school friend, as she could see me but I was surrounded by very tall people and hadn't been able to spot her, eventually a tannoy announcement was made for me to go to the desk where she was waiting. I had arranged to stay with Garth and Gregor for a few days for a reunion. They were working , so I was happy to rest after arriving and just have a walk round their area of Stoney Creek, that was when I discovered if you step off a pavement, sidewalk call it what you will, the cars stop as you have priority. I became more observant as didn't want to inconvenience people driving when I could wait till it was clear. It was great having a catch up, and other friends of theirs came for dinner one night which was great fun as the husband of that couple was a school mate from Primary school in Scotland, who had a butchers business in Hamilton and knew the old Aunt. While staying with them the weather warmed up and we were able to sit poolside in their garden and dip our toes into the water, quite a novelty for me.

A few days later I was picked up by Dorothy, one of the cousins, and taken to stay with Aunt Jenny, in Hamilton, Ontario, it was interesting finding my way about and eventually found the butcher shop, which was for any of the ex -pats a source of potato scones, plain bread, scotch pies, Cadbury chocolate. I returned with Aunt Jenny's shopping and a lot more which had been gifted as they wouldn't let me pay. The old school pals act!

Dorothy was still working as a teacher, but would pick us up after school, and took us to various places. One outstanding day was the trip to Niagara, which as we turned into the approach road and I got what I thought was my first glimpse, these turned out to be the American Falls, but I had exclaimed "Wow". Once we got parked up I could see the Canadian "real" version. While Aunt Jenny stayed in the car, Dorothy and I did the tunnels behind Niagara, which were made by Scottish miners who had gone out to Canada, which take you behind the falls, we then did the other tourist bit and wore the yellow rain capes and got the spray. I was not bothered about going onto the boat the "Maid of the Mist", as I was getting quite wet enough. It was absolutely stunning and we then had dinner at the Oban Inn at Niagara on the Lake. Tartan carpets everywhere, they liked their links with the Old Country! It was an excellent meal and Aunt Jenny insisted it was her treat. Another day we went to an Amish town called St. Jacob's and saw the most beautiful patchwork for sale, so some souvenirs were bought including beautiful patchwork quilting made into holders for lavender and also beautiful aprons, table runners, and of course bedspreads.

I had been told that the Amish did not want their photos taken so their wishes had to be respected. We were able to photograph their buggies and horses although not the people!

The handiwork and the quilting was superb, it was an amazing place to visit. The girls wore long plain dresses in pastel colours, maybe with a small floral print, and bonnets. The young men were dressed in their traditional old fashioned men's clothing but were smart, all the men wore hats! Black was the predominant colour for the males of the community.

Later driving around, Dorothy stopped and showed me a kissing bridge, so called as that covered bridge was where the young Amish could do their courting unseen. Who knows perhaps some others do too...

This was a place call West Montrose, another example of the British names taken with the people, to start their new lives. It amazed me all the names around Toronto, Hamilton, and Stoney Creek, which had links to the UK, but made me realise that emigres had taken their familiar names and architecture with them. Windsor, London, etc.

A few days later, her brother Ian and his wife Anita picked me up and took me into Toronto and gave me a tour. I was amazed at Yong Street which is the longest street in the World, and stretches from downtown Toronto to Algonquin Park Ontario, also the width of the streets. They took me to the CN Tower, where there is a glass floor which is strange to stand on, as you can see everything under your feet. We later went and met their other brother Doug and had a delicious dinner at a Greek Taverna.

They took me back to Aunt Jenny after that and I spent the evening telling her all that we had done.

The next day I got the bus into Toronto where Doug met me and took me to meet his friends, then we went for dinner at a Bistro, before going to a Blue Jays game. The roof of the stadium at that time was a new wonder as it could open and close, like many stadia now have, but then was innovative. It was an education seeing a Baseball game and I did my best to understand it, and Doug and his friend did their best to explain it to me. Thoroughly enjoyed it, especially as they won and the fireworks were set off at the end, and that only happens when they win a home game. Mike, Ian and Anita's son met me at Hamilton bus station and took me back to his Gran's flat.

One really entertaining day out with Aunt Jenny was when I was invited to accompany the seniors on their day out to, Cambridge Ontario, to a Safari Park. Little did I imagine when going to visit the family in Canada that I would spend a day with octogenarians, looking at Lions, Tigers, Hippos, Rhinos and other exotic animals. It was terrific, and one old man decided he wanted to be with me all day as he liked my West of Scotland accent as it reminded him of home long ago. They were a great bunch of old people.

All too soon, I had to bid farewell, and it was sad leaving Aunt Jenny, as I knew I wouldn't see her again. Later the family told me that my visit had really bucked her up, and she was better for a few months.

I am glad to say we saw the cousins again after that, and I still hope to pay a return visit to Canada!

Chapter 3

Laughter in Lanzarote!   And Merriment in Menorca!

The next holiday I did was with girlfriends as a group of four, and we went to Lanzarote, and hired a car, I was very brave and did the driving, the other pal who had said she would drive, was a bit unsure about this, so I was left with it, although she said she would maybe try later. There was another incident when bravery was called for as one day the friend I was sharing a room with shouted for me, I found her standing with her back to the wall nearly paralysed with fear, I asked what is it, she pointed to the floor where there was a cockroach. Quickest dispatch is crunch with the foot, but she couldn't move so I had to dispatch it for her. We immediately went to reception and got the spray to put round the skirting boards to keep them away. This is a hazard, of holidaying in warm places.

However, fairly early in the holiday when driving to Mirador del Rio, there was a stretch of road which is hairpin bends, my friend who could drive was in the passenger seat beside me, as she was still considering if she would have a shot, as her name was on the insurance, and the other two in the rear. All I could hear was the sharp and repeated intakes of breath, which was coming from the rear. It turned out one of the other girls suffered from vertigo and had been looking down, as we wound our way round these hairpin bends and were also descending very steeply. I wondered what on earth the matter was and it really did a lot for the confidence of the driver! The other added extra was that the road was virtually single track; yes it was tarred but had a fairly deep ditch at each side, and we are driving over a volcanic landscape black and rough, praying nothing would come the other way. The prickly pear growing were very pretty but I was more concerned with staying on the nice smooth bit and not having a mishap with the tyres leaving that and going off the sides. It was interesting to see the vineyards planted in the volcanic soil on the sides of the remains of the volcanic eruptions.

It was explained to us that any moisture is absorbed during the day and as it cools at night the plants get the benefit of this moisture, which is why this viniculture is successful. The vines are planted on terraces in the volcanic soil.

The Mirador del Rio was worth the white knuckles the view was beautiful. Another day we did a visit to Timanfaya to the volcano, and found that thin soles sandals were not ideal as the ground was pretty hot in places. We must have looked as though we were doing a disco dance, as we were jumping and hopping because of the hot ground. We saw the chicken pieces being cooked by the heat of the volcano, and sampled the volcanic barbequed chicken!

The beautiful sunshine was meaning we were going out and exploring and my confidence with the car was increasing. Finally before handing the car back we visited Cesar Manrique's house which comprises rooms made out of the air bubbles in the volcanic rock which he painted and furnished and lived in, a labyrinth of caves if you like but very comfortable and well worth seeing.

He was an architect and was instrumental in a law being brought in that buildings should not be taller than three storeys. There was a skyscraper in Arreciffe which was to have been demolished but I believe was eventually turned into a hotel, but all other buildings are of a traditional type, painted white and no more than three storeys high.

After giving up the car we went to see about a boat trip and went on a boat called Cesar II, which was going to Papagayo Beach, we thought great, swimming costumes and a swim at a beach, we were to get a lunch on the boat as well, it was a great trip and the lunch was a chicken and salad meal and perfectly adequate for the cost of the trip, however, on arriving at the beach, we were positively overdressed as when we got there discovered it was a nudist beach and we were all taken aback, however we had our swim wearing swimsuits, and then got back on the boat to return to Costa Teguise where we were staying. At that time Costa Teguise was relatively small and was being constructed as a custom built resort, but it had a certain charm, which later it lost. There was a particularly attractive restaurant down in the town with a lovely view of the beach which we frequented most evenings, as afterwards we could have a stroll along a promenade in the warm breeze. All in all it was a good holiday.

Merriment in Menorca

The next girly holiday was three years later and the destination this time was Menorca, to Cala Galdana with the same group. It was October and we realised once there the reason it was cheap was that our apartment was away up a high hill at the back of the town, at night it was a poorly lit road, and the more nervous amongst us were prone to squeals when any sudden sounds were heard. However we were having fun, and even swam in the pool a couple of times as it transpired we were the only residents in the block of apartments. It had been suggested that a car would be hired, but on the bus from the airport, the other would be driver spotted a guy standing beside his car about to get into it with his arm in plaster. No chance was she going to drive, if there were folk driving about in plaster. I agreed the bus would do fine and was sure we could manage.

Cala Galdana was a nice town with some lovely shops although it was the end of the season they were still well stocked. We found a wonderful shoe shop and all indulged our love of footwear, then went and had coffee and wandered back up later to our apartment.

We got about without any trouble on the buses, one day went into Mahon which involved changing buses, and had a wander about and looked at the shops. We found a bar overlooking the harbour and sat there for a couple of hours, as the shops shut for a siesta.

While there we saw a cruise shop was docked, and I realised it was the Saga Rose, and remarked I would love to go on that ship one day which when owned by Cunard was known as Vistafjord which was why my Mum liked it so much.

We chatted and when finishing our drinks waved to the passengers as the ship was starting its sail-away with the music playing. We gathered our stuff and went back to see if the shop which we particularly wanted to see was open again. By now it was starting to get chilly and having forgotten about shops closing for siesta we hadn't brought jackets with us. The shop was located; table cloth for our friend purchased, and then went for the bus. It took ages to come, and again we had to get off half way and wait for the next one going back to Cala Galdana. We were slightly on the cold side by the time we got back. We had decided that we would go down into the town for a meal, so set off all wearing our new shoes, and having jackets on so we wouldn't feel cold. We had a lovely meal and a walk along the prom at the edge of the shore then started to make our way back up the winding, long hill, when there was the most enormous crack of thunder, four bodies jumped in the air, and what we said was not printable, then torrential rain started. Fortunately we were level with a small bistro restaurant and dived into it as the proprietor came forward to put down a plastic awning to keep the rain off his outside tables. He indicated to us to sit and wait till the rain and thunder and lightning abated. We sat for ages, till eventually we thought we would be safe to continue our trek up the hill and round the bend to our abode. The road also was quite rough so with the poor lighting and the potholes we had to be careful. We set off and were only about ten minutes further up the road when it all fired off again, we hurried as best we could and were so pleased when we saw our door, spoke too soon, one friend in her new leather shoes did a fair imitation of Torvill and Dean and crashed down on the tiles in the patio area. So we got the door open got her inside and sat down with a cold compress on the already swelling ankle. Never any frozen peas when you need them! She was more concerned with her shoes and what they had cost, than with her ankle, but that is ladies who love shoes. We then got her dry clothes and helped her change, and got ourselves sorted out, including sweeping the water outside which had blown under the door into the apartment.

With the storm and the wind a couple of the party thought that there was someone else in the apartments and that the door was being tried, as there was banging. I said no, I didn't think so, but to reassure them said how about after locking the door, we put a chair under the handle and just leave some stuff in the middle of the floor so when it is dark there is a trip hazard. That seemed to do the trick and we went off to bed. It transpired that the maids when cleaning had opened the shutters and forgotten to close them, so in the wind they were banging and it sounded like someone banging on the door. That is the worst of vivid imaginations. The next day we thought we would just have a quiet day, and as it was a lovely sunny day, we went round to the pool. One of my friends lay on a lounger and read a book while the rest of us went swimming, when one of the other two started to have difficulty as she was out her depth, we shouted to our friend who was reading and was oblivious to this, and was not responding so the two of us had to dive under our friend and push her to the surface, and shout again, when thank goodness she dropped her book and came and helped us. We told our not so good swimmer to stay at the shallow end and not to frighten us like that again. I sat for a little while reading my book and had put my glasses on, I then went back in the water and forgot I had my glasses on and they sank to the bottom of the pool, and of course I couldn't see them, so my bookworm friend dived down and got them for me, quite an exciting afternoon.

The next day we decided as it was sunny but not warm enough now for the pool, so get the bus and go to Cuitadella. What a pretty place, we had a wander and found our way down to the harbour. There were a multitude of restaurants, and the biggest problem was deciding which menu we liked best. We eventually settled on a place with fish specialities and sat and had our meal and enjoyed the view. After lunch we just had a wander about and bought some pictures to bring home as souvenirs.

.

The next day we had time after packing up to go to the beach and have a paddle in the warm sea before going to the airport. It was a lovely holiday with good company.

Chapter 4

Just for a Day

In 1997 my friend Audrey and I saw a day trip to Prague advertised from Glasgow. We thought that's for us, as my son was working there at the time, so we had arranged that we would try and meet him at lunch time once our tour was over. This was to be on the 3rd of June so we thought nice day out. We had to be at the airport at 5am and met with the rest of the group. We waited and waited and there were a couple of well-known TV news presenters in the group, so as it became evident there was a problem there was grumbling and they vanished after it was announced the trip was cancelled due to technical problem with the plane. There was a lot of anger and the poor rep was having a terrible time. We said to her it's not your fault, so we arranged to get picked up and taken home and they said they would try to reschedule and let us know. Some people were shouting for compensation, as though that could be dealt with there and then. It turned out that the replacement plane was at Manchester and there was no way they could bring it to Glasgow and get us to Prague with anything like enough time to give us a tour and the free time needed. Needless to say due to our illustrious TV presenters it was all over the news later that day. I contacted the company and sent a letter to say no way did the reps handle it badly, it was purely circumstances out with their control.

A couple of weeks later we got a letter offering a full refund of the £147 plus the chance to go just paying the airport taxes. We said yes please we will go, I didn't take my refund as by this time my son had come home, and I offered him the chance to go so he could show us round as previously arranged, and meet up with his friends. So the three of us now set off and were at the airport at 5am. Now Audrey had just got engaged that weekend and the day of the trip was her birthday, Tuesday 19th August, so she was in great form. As we were going to departures this guy came up and put his arms round our shoulders and said "Have a great day girls" in what can only be described as a fake American accent. It was her fiancé giving her a surprise. That was dedication at that time of the morning. Our trip went ahead totally to plan, and we had our tour, which son agreed with reps he would skip as knew the city, saw Charles Bridge in the rain, and the artists trying to keep their work dry. It was a good walking tour although it was very wet. Some people had the presence of mind to bring umbrellas, but we had thought August no… Audrey did have a rain jacket, but she is more sensible than me. I am always thinking it won't rain.

At lunch time we met up with my son and his friend as arranged at the Astronomical Clock, which is a wonderful clock with an amazing and tragic story as to how it was made, and then the maker was killed so he couldn't made another one like it. We were then taken to the restaurant where my son had been working, which was down the narrow opening to the left of the Our Lady before Tyn Church with its two towers directly across from the Clock and met some of the people he had worked with including an American girl called Autumn. I had never met anyone before with the name of a season which suited her as she had the most gorgeous auburn hair.

We were given T shirts as souvenirs they only did one size Enormous! We had lovely steak for lunch, and the boss seemed to be pleased to see my son again. I tried to find the restaurant years later when attending a wedding of a son of another friend, and found a bar/restaurant in the same place, they thought it may have been called Oscars at one time. The boys then took us on what can only be described once over Charles Bridge, as a pub crawl, well for them as they kept vanishing. However before that happened we saw a lovely little shop just over the other side of Charles Bridge and went in for a look, and they had a set of four beautiful crystal glasses for Becherovka, which I had been persuaded to try after lunch. It is described as a digestif not unpleasant but very strong almost a schnaps. I let my boy discuss the price of these and then I bought the set and also got a gorgeous little crystal bell, I still have the glasses and bell. I still hope I got local rate as he had learned to speak Czech, the bottle of Becherovka which I bought as a souvenir, has been consumed and is now a lamp!

We then climbed and climbed up hundreds of steps with a stop at Molly Malone's an Irish Pub. The settee we sat on had long lost its springs so we were sitting in a huge hollow; it was very dimly lit and hilarious, very atmospheric, forget Molly Malone more Dracula! I recollect a lot of Staropramen beer being consumed by said young lads and a couple by us, the boys were hilarious and we were being extremely careful as Audrey and I were having a ball, and having had lunch with wine and trying Becherovka, and spending time taking lots of photos we knew we had to get back to the bus on time and tried to impress this on my son who was travelling back with us. We then continued up these hundreds of steps, stopped for a photo (breather), and finally got to

St. Vitus Cathedral, which took 1000 years to build (930 – 1930) and was completed to its original plans. I also understand that there could be a few years leeway in the thousand years, as referred to in the installation of stained glass.

This is all built within the confines of the castle. Also at this elevated height we have the Palace the residence of the President, with the soldiers in pale blue uniforms, we were there when they were changing the guard, not quite the same as Buckingham Palace, but still worth seeing.

Once at the top you see the enormity of St. Vitus Cathedral!

At this point there is nowhere to step backwards to get the magnificence of it in the viewfinder on the camera. Remember this is 1997 pre mobile phones. So short of lying on your back on wet paving it was that! However we settled for just the doorway that gives an indication of the beauty of this building, and then took a photo of the top of the building.

The stained glass was not installed until the 1930's when the building was finished. It is beautiful. It was a whistle stop visit. We then worked our way back down through little streets and saw Franz Kafka's house, which was tiny. The view of the city on the way back gave a greater idea of the size of it. I now realise the difference digital makes as then we were still putting film into a camera and printing these off via a chemist shop.

We had been told to be at the Intercontinental Hotel by 5.00pm to get the coach back to the airport. Well Audrey and I were there, but son and pal had gone off to see someone else after we were making our way back down, and time was getting tight. I was starting to panic when a car raced up and the bold boy got out. It was obvious there had been a fair bit of celebration going on. However we piled onto the coach and headed with everyone accounted for to the airport. As we approached the airport we stopped and were in a queue of coaches. The reason was explained, there was a flight for Israel taking off and while that was in progress all traffic near the airport was stopped till it was up and away. We then got into the airport, and were checked in for our charter flight. Once on board, we were given refreshments, Audrey was then approached by the stewardess who that morning had found out it was Audrey's birthday, and Audrey had said she had just got engaged. Audrey to her delight was invited onto the flight deck, and was thrilled. That wouldn't happen now. We got home at 10.30pm to Glasgow and were picked up after an excellent day out. People didn't believe us when we said we had gone to Prague for the day from Glasgow.

Chapter   5

My Millennium Experience - Journey to the end of the World.

My real introduction to long haul was due to my intrepid mother deciding to go on a cruise to Antarctica and needing rescued from Tierra del Fuego.

In December 1999 when my mother, who was 87, said she was going to do a trip to Antarctica my reaction was she must be off her head, and I remarked to my husband that I would end up having to go and get her one way or another. I said this when we were visiting a cousin in Dumfries. I never realised how prophetic my words would be.

Monday 10th January 2000 I received a telephone call from Lucy at Saga Welfare, advising me that my mother was ill on board the Marco Polo. Her condition was described as having flu and pneumonia, weak but just stable. The Marco Polo having just been to Antarctica was still two days from port at Ushuaia. I spent the next few days in a state of optimism, pessimism, fear and desperation to get to her. Lucy from Saga was excellent and kept in daily contact sometimes more than once to keep me informed. The message coming through was that she was too ill to be airlifted, and also the location made this difficult if not impossible.

My main problem was that my Dad who was 92 had to be told, but only when positive steps were in place as to how this situation was going to be resolved, this advice coming from the family doctor. By this time I had indicated that I would be willing to go, and another family friend had also said that if need be she would go.

I was going, then I was not, but a nurse would be sent, then again I was going, and so on until I got word at 17.45 on the 12th January that I was going the next day and Worldwide Assistance in London were arranging tickets for me and I had to get travel insurance. As I was being given one way tickets this had to be a year policy. Within half an hour Saga had this in place for me. My

Dad took me to a travel agent in Saltcoats to get dollars so I had money.

The Thursday was spent getting a bag sorted out and dollar traveller cheques. My husband and my Dad came with me to Glasgow airport, and I collected my first two air tickets. These got me as far as Buenos Aires. I found the flight to London a slight strain, and just before we got there was finding it very difficult to concentrate on keeping myself together. I told a steward why and from then on British Airways did everything they could to help me. I was taken a quick way to International Departures, and they checked that there was nothing for me to collect there at Gatwick, as I had been led to believe that an insurance document might be there. I got onto the Buenos Aires flight and within five minutes was asked if I was alright to which I answered no, they thought I was afraid of flying, so I said no, I was afraid my mother might die before I got there. Within five minutes I had been taken and put into Club Class, where I was gently asked periodically if I was alright and did I need anything. They gave me extra pillows and blankets. I managed to get some sleep, which helped enormously, and in the morning a stewardess came and asked me if I was feeling better. They had someone at Buenos Aires to help me through immigration, and to help me get the travellers cheques cashed and to buy a ticket for the bus to the Jorge Newbery airport. She also took me to the bus and told me to stay on it till it stopped at the other airport. By this time I was melting as the temperature in Buenos Aires was 21 degrees and I had left Scotland in winter!

The bus took us through Buenos Aires and this was interesting, as some of the buildings are magnificent, there are also distinct signs of extreme poverty. The journey took one hour.

After that I really was on my own, I got to Jorge Newbery airport, and had to go and ask for my ticket, which was when the lack of knowledge of Spanish hit me, I had my Dad's pocket dictionary so was looking up words and pronouncing them badly but got understood. I got the tickets, and had to phone the Assistance people in London, so had to go into a booth and make the call, then, pay for it. I mistakenly handed over money before going in and then handed over more when asked when I came out however it was not a lot of money to have misused, and I tried to get the man in London to understand that it was not going to be easy to phone. He thought everyone spoke English in Argentina. I put through a call to Worldwide Assistance and spoke to Sebastian, who had been the contact I had heard from at home. I seemed to pay for it twice as the woman who gave me five dollars change from my ten dollars then asked me for another ten and gave me five dollars change. I couldn't argue as the call had been $5.64 and therefore the problem was arising as I didn't have the 64 centavos, it had to be the correct money.

I had been told that at Ushuaia there were not many facilities. OK but what and what not?

After that I went to the rest room and got myself a T shirt out and did a quick change, so now had a coat to carry as well as a bag, it was the suede coat I had bought in Portugal several years earlier and was heavy, and I was travelling light with just hand luggage! I had not been thinking that this was their summer and I was wearing my winter clothes, Buenos Aires was warm!

Eventually I discovered a lounge/café upstairs where I could get coffee as I had five hours till my next flight left. I quickly ascertained that nobody seemed to speak much if any English, and those that perhaps did I hadn't found. At this point I had asked the insurance people to let my family know that I was fine, as my father was convinced that if I went in a taxi unless I knew they were reputable I would disappear, so the phone call although complicated let them know I was OK. I did at this point say I didn't know when I would be able to phone again, as the language was proving a problem.

At one point the activity in the airport increased as the Argentine Rugby team arrived with the accompanying television cameras, reporters, and fans. It was interesting to watch as they had Mothers, Fathers, wives and babies too; they all kissed each other, and took photos with the fans. The whole place came to a standstill till they had gone through to the departure lounge.

I decided that I should get some more currency as all I had was the small amount I had got at Ezezia Airport to get the bus, and I was starting to wonder what facilities there would be at Ushuaia. I couldn't find anything that resembled a currency exchange. Shortly afterwards a lady asked me what I thought of the airport in Spanish and as I had replied I spoke English, she then asked in English, and I took the opportunity to ask if she knew where I could change money. She was pleased to be able to help me, and showed me where it was.

Eventually the flight was called, and I went through to a basic departure lounge and walked across the tarmac to board a plane, praying I had got this right, as everything was in Spanish. Four hours after boarding we came in to land at Ushuaia and my first impression was where was the airstrip, as we circled and banked steeply, then circled again all the time getting quite low over the water, but no glimpse of an airport. First sight of the town gave me the feeling that I was looking at somewhere similar to photos I had seen of the Falkland Islands. This given the location was not surprising. I realised then that this was Ushuaia,

Tierra del Fuego, Fin del Mundo.

I admit I was relieved when I felt the plane touch down, it wasn't till later that I realised there was really quite a distance to the mountains, they had just seemed very close, and we had been circling tightly as the area we were in was the border of Argentina and Chile. I suppose being under stress and knowing we were so near I was anxious to get into the terminal and get on my way to the clinic. It was by this time 18.30 on Friday 14th January. There is a three hour time difference. I also didn't know that the letter H is silent and the letter J should be said like H.

I managed to ask for a taxi to take me to the clinic where my mother was. First snag no phone to make an international call. Second snag was when I got to the clinic no one understood what I was trying to ask, which was "please take me to Senora McInnes", partly the fact no English spoken and mostly my lack of their language Spanish! For a short time I wondered if I was in the wrong clinic, or worst case scenario! Eventually the girl I was trying to speak to, left me and went to get a man, who it transpired, was the radiologist, who had some English and he took me upstairs to my Mum. Until I got into her room and actually saw her I was very apprehensive or what I was going to find. He asked me which hotel I was staying at, so I explained that I had been told that the clinic would help me either find somewhere or let me stay there. He then went and found another man who could understand English and between them they agreed that I could stay with my mother. They then arranged this and got Mum to another room which had a settee, which they made up as a bed for me. This was fun especially at 2.00am each night when they came to check on Mum, and the phrase was "disculpme" excuse me. I could not, and never would, fault their care of my mother, it was superb. I was learning new words in the middle of the night!

This was when my new form of communication had to improve rapidly. The nurses soon learned to ask me where my "libro" or "dictionario" was, as none of them spoke English. Even the girls who brought the food started to teach me new words each day. How to tell someone it was all right to come into the room, which the girl said, was "adelante", she showed me by knocking on the door and then saying the word, also how to say I was going for a walk, I used "andar" which is the verb and wiggled my fingers in the walking signal! Worldwide Assistance had by this time guaranteed payment at the clinic, as Visa was not accepted, my mother's card was Visa. It is definitely a cash society; hotels and some of the shops take travellers cheques. Mastercard was more acceptable as the banks will pay on Mastercard but not always on Visa or Amex. There were signs everywhere, the downside being they were in Spanish!

Saturday dawned, and as I wasn't at all sure I would get food for myself at the Clinic, I thought I should explore and find my options. I had been told there was a restaurant, which was the canteen, but not having been able to find it, and not being able to ask with English being in short supply, I walked into the town to find out what was there. I found the ships agent office, and managed to identify myself to one of the men there, who took a photocopy of my passport and tried to give me tickets for Mr. and Mrs. Fisher, who were involved with the clinic and also had been on the Marco Polo. I then found a restaurant where the original shop in the town had been, and got myself some chicken and vegetables. It was ordered using a dictionary and pointing to the menu. I had first of all asked for "Polo" which is an ice lolly, not the "Pollo" which is chicken. I tried to explain to the man that I didn't speak Spanish and was here because my mother was ill. He eventually did a chicken impersonation along the lines of flapping his elbows and going a "pechoook" sound, the deal was done I got a chicken dinner.

I was so delighted I was able to ask for the coffee! My one phrase "Café solo por favor" The arrangement of bottles and ornaments were fascinating, I would have liked to have studied them longer. I think he was quite pleased that I had liked his restaurant. I walked back to the clinic, along Avenida Maipu, and found booths advertising trips. When I got back to the clinic I showed these to Mum who insisted that I must see as much of the place as I could while she was still in the clinic. I then discovered Mum had the most enormous plate of food which under normal circumstances she would never manage to eat. So we cut it up and got her to eat a little, and I ate some of it working on the theory I didn't know where or when I would get another meal. This soon became evident as that night another huge plateful arrived for her, so I shared her food and ate standing up at the side of her bed. Plastic forks from aeroplanes are useful. I never did find the canteen in the Clinic, but if I had started falling over from hunger I dare say I would have been directed to it. On the Sunday the Clinic had presented me with an envelope with Mother's X-Rays and informed us that she was to leave the Clinic and go to a hotel the next day. As she was at this time still on a drip, and other medications I could not see how this could be. This again was due to the member of staff who thought the way to speak English to me was to shout at me, she was actually quite good, but Mum got a bit upset at the shouting, despite the lack of a hearing aid! I think it was enthusiasm in retrospect. I do hope now the lady in question has mastered our most difficult language, as I am still trying to master Spanish! Fortunately this proved to be wrong as it was another couple of days before the subject rose again. I can only guess that this was in part due to Mr. Fisher being discharged, and they had the idea that we were all together, given Mum and the two of them were of the Marco Polo!

I decided to go to the museum and walked into the town, and spent time in the Museo Fin del Mundo, and bought a book for Mum and Dad, and a penguin badge for myself.

This is a most interesting Museum showing early life in Tierra del Fuego, and had cases with stuffed birds which showed some varieties now rare. Mum said she would like a penguin badge, so as Mr and Mrs Fisher had left the Clinic and had left a note with their room number at their hotel, I said I would walk in again, and try and see Mr. and Mrs. Fisher. There was no problem at the Museum about going in to get Mum a penguin badge, as the girl remembered me and I managed to explain I wanted to buy more souvenirs. Unfortunately I couldn't get the Fishers as they were not in their room.

Monday morning, I felt confident enough to ask the clinic to phone Tamic and they sent someone to take me to a phone house as they referred to it, this is these cabins where you phone and then pay after, so could phone Worldwide and tell them why I had been unable to call.

Tamic the ship's agents insisted that they weren't obliged to help us as my mother had been a passenger and they were responsible for crew. However, they agreed, as we were so far from home, that if we needed help we should ask and they would try to help.

They sent me to a bank where I would be able to cash the travellers' cheques, wrong bank, but one man spoke some English, so he gave me directions. I was told to go back one block to the territorial bank.

I went to the other bank and was served by Oriano Tati, I tried speaking in Spanish, and he said he knew some English and would like to practice. This was amazing to find two people in ten minutes who did speak some English. When I had to go back and cash my mother's cheques for her a couple of days later, I stood in the queue and hoped that when my turn came it would be Oriano who would be free. I did notice that some people had stepped aside, obviously wanting the same. He was the person for the wages cheques and the travellers' cheques. We exchanged email addresses!

While I was in the town I went to see about the trip to Estancia Harberton. Due to the weather it was not leaving by boat from Ushuaia at 10.00am but by land at 14.00.

 The Yamanas were nomadic people and built these little houses, conical ones almost like igloos but made out of tree branches, and left when they moved on there was also a little hump in front of these where the shells and husks from seafood, and seeds would be discarded outside of the door. I saw a replica when on the trip to the ranch.

When I got back to the clinic my mother told me my husband had phoned the clinic and had spoken to her. She told him why we hadn't been able to phone. Worldwide had phoned my husband to ask if he had heard from me, no one had thought that if I hadn't phoned to phone the clinic. Worldwide had not understood what I was trying to say from Buenos Aires.

Mum had saved me a chicken fillet as she had again had a large plate of food. So lunch was taken care of. Mum kept telling me to hurry so I wouldn't be late.

We were taken overland by mini bus and the scenery was beautiful. I met a lady from New York, Helen, and as she and I were the only English speakers on the trip, we got a guide to ourselves. It was a most interesting trip, and we got taken round the conservation area to see all the different trees and plants. The garden at the house was like an old English garden, with fuchsias, lupins, broom, delphiniums, primulas, and the most gorgeous old fashioned scented roses. We also saw in the shearing shed and had the shearing process explained to us. Helen stayed at the house, and looked round it, as she said she was going on a ship and would see penguins. This house was shipped out from Bristol and arrived in pieces and had to be assembled, on the land given by the Argentine government to Thomas Bridges to thank him for his work with the native people.

It seemingly has had an upstairs added to it, but still has the corrugated iron roofing which was on the original structure. A lot of the older buildings still have corrugated iron roofing.

I went on a zodiac to see the penguins, and was only sorry I ran out of film as a King penguin appeared with the other smaller ones. Helen and I met up when I got back and had the most delicious cakes and tea. Travelling back in the minibus we had an Italian man for company, who spoke Italian and as Helen spoke English and Spanish and a little Italian, and I was still at the stage I was mostly speaking English with an odd word of Spanish we had a circular conversation, he would ask something in Italian, Helen would tell me in English and then reply to him for both of us.

On the Tuesday I went to the Maritime Museum, but discovered that even in the cold climate of the south siesta hours are observed. A boy of about ten insisted on speaking to me and tried to show me another door for the museum: I was puzzled as to why he wasn't at school! It was later someone said that it was the summer holiday. Eventually that figured as opposite hemisphere! They were running about in shirtsleeves, and I had a jacket on. I walked back into the town and met two Swedish girls and a girl from London, so we all ended up sitting outside a café wearing our warm jackets having our coffee and talking English. They had been on the trip on the Russian ship to Antarctica. I then walked back to the clinic and found a supermarket and went and bought myself some crisps and lemonade so I could snack while reading my book, which fortunately I had brought a thick one in English, as all the books in the shops were in Spanish.

Wednesday morning we got a visit from Dr. Cronin, the ship's doctor, who had come to the clinic with a crew member, and as Tamic told him we were still there he came up to see Mum. It was lovely to be able to thank him for looking after Mum. His driver from Tamic was with him and this was the man who had gone to the ship with his minibus to get Mum to the clinic. This was my first meeting with Louis Alberto Lazo.

I had also discovered a chemist shop where the pharmacist spoke some English and on my second visit he said he had seen me in the Bank. I think the Scottish lady whose mother was ill in the Clinic was being watched to see she was getting on all right!

Patricia Lorenzo one of the nurses wanted me to go home with her for a meal, but that would have involved leaving mother in the clinic, she had by this time shown signs or worry if I was away too long. It was lovely to have been asked. One day I thought I had lost a small souvenir I had bought for my sons and when Patricia found out she got her mother to go and buy me another one and bring it to the Clinic. That is an example of how kind these people are and how much they look after visitors to their Island. She and I became very adept at looking up the dictionary quickly. We developed and mime and language communication. The people are hard -working and kind and in the clinic the nurses were superb, loving, and gentle, and although my mother couldn't understand a word being spoken to her she was content in the care she was receiving. Part of her problem with hearing was that she had left her hearing aid at home on the dining room table, and as I hadn't realised that I hadn't taken it with me.

I learnt more Spanish by the day in an attempt to keep communication levels at the maximum. There were a couple of people at the Clinic who had a reasonable level of English but they were not always accessible. One of them tried hard, although her English was like my Spanish we persevered. Once I finished my book I gave it to her to help her with her English. At this time they were not teaching English in the schools.

Through conversation with my mother from early after my arrival we were able to heal thirty years and probably longer, of misunderstanding that had led to a definite coolness in our relationship. It was a shame that my mother was ill, and had been so very ill, but if that had not happened this reconciliation would not have either.

During the journey to Harberton and talking to Helen, she had asked why I was on my own, was I like her travelling alone? I told her why I was there and that I had wondered how my mother would react to me coming and why. She then told me she was a psychotherapist and could reassure me that this was one great chance for reaching an understanding which had been getting missed for a number of years! This it proved to be!

On the Wednesday we met again by chance, as after being at the Bank for Mum, I had met again an Italian man who had been on our trip to the Ranch at Harberton. He had spoken to me earlier, and when Helen came along he had told her that Senora de Escosia, had gone up the street. He had been instructed by Helen to keep me talking till she got back. However as I was now able to understand that he was telling me she was two minutes up the street I had just come down, I did an about turn, and went off to find her. We ended up in a café drinking more of the black coffee we both enjoyed. She was so pleased to hear the rest of the story. I told her that I was happy as Mum and I had talked through our hurt and misunderstandings, and Mum was equally happy we had been able to do this. To happen anywhere would have been wonderful, but somehow there it gave everything an added poignancy. Perhaps it was because we had no distractions, we both knew it could have ended so very differently and perhaps it was one of these situations where you feel it was meant to happen. How glad I am that instinct made me want to go. Ushuaia will always be a very special place to me and I think also to my mother. Love and care surrounded us from complete strangers; we found we could talk to each other again and were in amongst the most spectacular scenery. How many people get this chance?

My mother now appreciated how ill she must have been, but she got where she wanted and completed an almost thirty year journey which took her to 80 degrees north, Longyearbyen, round the world three times, and finally the day she took ill, she stood on Deception Island in

Antarctica. She also had walked on the Great Wall in China. Few 87 year old ladies have done that! Helen was joining the Russian ship to go to Antarctica, so we bade farewell, and have promised to keep in touch. Helen visited me in Scotland a few years later and was able to meet my Mum and brought a lovely pastel picture she had done of her interpretation of Antarctica and was given to my mother as a memento of a shared experience.

Ushuaia still has a pioneering feel about it although it does have souvenir shops. It is quite a large town; I was told population is about 40,000. It is the most southern town in the world. It is 620 miles from Antarctica.

After leaving Helen, it was the opening time for the Museo Maritimo, y Presidio, the Maritime Museum and Old Prison. This was very interesting, as upstairs they have photographs from other Prison Museums of the World, and there were pictures of Inverary Prison Museum, in Scotland, although they had it labelled as Irlanda! There was also a room showing what the original Post Office was like, and stuffed penguins and seals. That let me find out that the penguins I had seen were Magellan penguins.

The old cells were depicting various scenarios and there was one which was about Scott of the Antarctic also other Antarctic Expeditions. This was a very interesting way to spend time. On the way back to the clinic I went shopping again, this time to get some more nightwear for Mum as the washing facilities were the hand basin in the room and the shower, both for us and any smalls. I found a shop selling ladies wear, and did not have my dictionary with me so with mime and a lot of hilarity got the shop assistants to understand what I was looking for. They brought out garments which would fit me, so I had to mime that "mi Madre grande!" They got the message and produced suitable nighties. This is quite an educational journey! Later I went to get a fleecy jacket as I was finding the coat I had brought a bit heavy, and got one with a pattern of a compass on the back, Mum had

said I was to get something to take home, so got a
couple of T shirts as well. The lady in the shop was very
helpful, and asked if I was on holiday in Spanish but as I
was picking up bits I had managed to get a little phrase
or two sorted out to explain to people, that it was
because Mum was ill. Each day there would be a call
from Lucy at Saga, to check everything was all right,
even at the weekend she got someone else to phone just
so we had contact with them. It was good to know we
had back up albeit thousands of miles away.

Chapter 6

From the End of the World back to the Northern
Hemisphere!

We next were told on the Thursday 20th that we were to
go to a hotel for lunchtime, we asked the clinic to phone
Tamic and arrange the minibus to take us. Of course we
got another huge envelope with more X-rays to bring
home. Luis Alberton arrived at 17.30 to take us to the
Hotel Cambio, where, after he had got Mum in the door
we discovered that it had fifteen steps to the bedrooms
and no lift. So Luis Alberto Lazo took over and phoned
Tamic and was then instructed to take us to the
mountain. We drove round Pharmacies first to get the
prescriptions for Mum, and then up and out from the
town till we reached the Hotel Del Glacier, which is
perched under the Glacier Martial, and has the most
incredible view of Ushuaia, and across the Beagle
Channel.

The two waitresses Bettina and Claudia who helped me with my Spanish were very kind, and also wanted me to go to their house for a lamb dinner, but I had to check on Mum regularly, and could not be out the hotel or she would worry, so apologised that I had to stay in the hotel. I am still in touch with Bettina.

Once I got Mum settled in our room, I went back downstairs to see a receptionist Roxanne who said she stayed in the Hotel and to ask for her if I needed help. I explained to her what was going on and after having a bit of a weep, she sat me down, got me some water, and chatted to me until I got myself gathered together. She agreed that it had been a very worrying situation to be in so far from home. The Hotel we were staying in is at the top of a long and winding road with no pavement which is why the help of Luis Alberto was proving so important to get me into town and back again, as the road was not safe to walk.

While I was at the Hotel with my mother, Luis Alberto sent a driver to take me to the town when I needed things for Mum. I managed to pay for that trip. Again when it became evident that a visit to the clinic was needed to get them to contact Worldwide, Jorge Miguel the son in law of Luis Alberto was sent to take me. At this point the Clinic indicated that they thought we had already gone back to Scotland, Jorge Miguel came in with me and although he didn't speak English I had been able make him understand what I needed done. He told me that the clinic now understood, he then took me to a supermarket to get some biscuits and things to help tempt my mother to eat. I was looking for tea biscuits and was trying to explain to him what they were, when he started to make a buzzing noise and waving his arms in a flying movement. He pointed to some biscuits and I realised he was telling me they were honey biscuits. Needless to say I bought them as they looked similar to tea biscuits.

He refused to let me pay for the trip to the town. They seemed to have appointed themselves our protectors. Only once in the second week was I asked for payment for the return journey, and it was not either Luis or Miguel, although the guy had been told to wait and bring me back and did.

The next day we got word that we were to fly home, this was the 26th of January, and I was to get a certificate of fitness to fly for my mother from the Clinic. The hotel phoned the clinic who said to phone again at 14.00, so they did and were told to phone again at 15.00 as the doctor would be there, at 15.00 they phoned again and were told to phone at 16.00 as the doctor would be there by then. Same thing at 16.00, 16.30 and 17.00 at which time they also said if I came to the Clinic for 18.00 the doctor would be there to see his patients, so Luis Alberto was phoned to come and get me at the hotel, which he did, and then came into the Clinic with me and stayed till we got the certificate at 18.30. This being totally in Spanish was a mystery to me but certainly did the trick, when shown at the airport.

Luis Alberto then took me on a tour of the town, to see his son, daughter in–law and grand-daughter, so I could say goodbye to them. Then we went back to the Hotel where he came to say goodbye to Mum, as it was his day off when we were to go to the Airport. So he gave me a bit of paper to give to the driver of the minibus who would come.

On the Thursday after we had tried with my improved Spanish to tell the hotel management and staff how we felt about the support and kindness they had shown, we were sitting in reception waiting when Luis Alberto came in, Mum was thrilled. He had taken her from the ship to the Clinic, the Clinic to the Hotel, and was now taking her to the Airport. He was so gentle with her, lifted her into the minibus and then swung her seat round so she had no extra effort to get into the minibus.

We got to the airport and met the lady who had sold me my jacket. I recognised her face but couldn't work out how, so she hugged me, patted my jacket and pointed to my T shirt, then asked how my Mama was, but this time I could understand most of what she was saying, so showed her where Mum was sitting waiting in a wheelchair, so she then said she would stand with our bags till I got Mum across to the bags. Luis Alberto had said Adios to us, but had said he would be back. Unfortunately before he came back we were taken for boarding, but as email is world-wide I have sent him a thank you as best I can.

We also got a chance to say thank you to Edel from Tamic who had done his best to help me as he was also at the airport. We flew back with Aerolineas Argentina to Buenos Aires. While we were waiting to get a voucher for a taxi transfer, it was Mum who was overdressed as we had made sure she was warm. As she had on an angora polo-neck, and a cardigan, she was overheating, so the two men with the wheelchair helped to hold her cardigan round her while I whipped off her jumper, and nearly took her specs too. We got our taxi transfer for us to Ezezia where we got an Iberian flight to Madrid.

The driver took us to the wrong terminal, and by this time we were in it with Mum propped up on the luggage trolley while I tried to get hold of help and a wheelchair. We were shortly afterwards loaded on a road train type vehicle and taken over to the correct terminal. Mum could sit in the vehicle and the driver went off to get the wheelchair. Once at the correct terminal we blithely sallied forth to get the tickets which were pre-booked. Manana – Yes we were on the computer list for the flight, but the tickets were not ready.

A young man came and painstakingly hand wrote out the tickets not only to Madrid, but also for Madrid to London, and London to Glasgow. I was desperate for a coffee and a sandwich. By this time we had a security man to wheel Mum who bless him also periodically carried my bag for me. We worked our way up a huge queue to get our passports stamped and our certificate of entry taken back. Then we were waved forwards as they spotted the wheelchair and we got queue jumping, and then Mum was taken up in a lift and I walked the stairs, with my bag! Once at the top I waited for Mum and her chair pusher, and although he spoke no English, he knew we wanted the café and the duty free shop. So those taken care of he then pushed Mum till I took her to "el bañó", the toilet. He waited with all our bags for us, then we reloaded Mum and he took us to the departure lounge.

The only snag on the flight to Madrid was the man across the aisle snoring, but eventually he dropped off properly, and we both got some sleep. I had in the meantime trotted up and back on the plane to ask the stewardesses for hot water in a cup for Mum, as that seemed to help her, and compared to the British Airways staff they were less than attentive to someone who was supposed to be on an assisted repatriation journey. Again at Madrid it was hot, and there we had forty minutes between the flights, to get through immigration and re-board another Iberia plane to London Heathrow. Heathrow was easy as we could now speak English and be understood; British Midland put us in the Executive Lounge to wait for our flight to Glasgow. That transfer was delayed as the bridge they had requested to board Mum from the tarmac was at another plane, so we had a lengthy wait. They then had to take us into the plane from the opposite side to the steps access, as they were still in place. All other passengers had boarded, and our seats were at the back of the plane, no one had thought if an assisted passenger was coming aboard it would be easier to be at the front. There were several mutterings as to the flight being delayed and it being due to us not being on time, I did not hesitate and said sorry but this was not down to us, that as we had travelled for 28 hours without a break, and it was not our fault the bridge had not been put in place in time, and was totally out-with our control. I think once many of the passengers had seen this elderly lady struggle to the back of the plane they realised it was not an excuse!

We had made all our connections but my mother's small case didn't!

We arrived at Glasgow where a Saga lady called Maureen met us, which was just as well as the pre-ordered taxi failed to show up. So she went and organised a taxi to take us to West Kilbride, where we got home to just after midnight, absolutely shattered.

The next day the small case caught up with us, and was delivered by taxi!

Worldwide Assistance helps people all over the world many of them in remote place, the only problem I had with them was convincing them that these people didn't understand that faxes should be replied to. Manana rules, but that same manana gave us a week in a hotel to let my mother get stronger. It also gave me time to learn some Spanish and gave me time with some exceptionally kind people.

Since coming home I have spoken to Lucy and Sebastian and hope that they really understood how much I appreciated them being there.

I also contacted British Airways to let them know how kind and helpful the crew on the flights from Glasgow, London and Madrid had been, praise where it is due. I also did not slate the flights back where help was less than I had hoped for, as I think there may have been a lack of understanding due to less urgency and translation!

The coincidences continued within a couple of weeks of getting home. After finishing a game of curling and sitting in the lounge at the ice rink with fellow team members, and our opposing team, the conversation was about my trip. One of the team had asked me to bring my photographs, so everyone was having a look at them. A lady in the other team said she had a story about Patagonia, and proceeded to tell me that her husband's grandfather who belonged to Ardrossan, (five miles from my home) had been the Captain on the "Glencairn", which had been shipwrecked at Cape Horn, and rescued by the Yamana Indians.

The Indians had taken the seafarers to a mission run by Lucas Bridges. She also said that Lucas Bridges wife had come from Troon, also in Ayrshire near where we live. Thomas Bridges, Lucas Bridges' father built Estancia Harberton. He had started the mission in

Ushuaia. Harberton was the village in Devon where Thomas' wife had come from, which is near Plymouth.

I had read about this in the museum, and also was told about it during my visit to Harberton. Small world isn't it! I am sure that I was meant to go there. I felt at home with the scenery, and the people. Senora simpatico, I was told, when struggling to say what I meant in Spanish.

I left a little of my heart in Ushuaia and ate a calafete berry, which legend says if you do you will return.

Chapter 7

Surprises from the USA

The next surprise I got, after that trauma, was an email one night from a cousin in America, saying that she and her cousin had been discussing the fact that I had gone to Argentina and had to stay for two weeks till I could get Mum home, and they had come up with a plan. I was to be sent tickets to go there for a holiday, and would spend one week with one cousin and her husband who would show me round their part of New England, and then we would all gather again at Buzzard Bay for a weekend, before they had to return to work and she would take me to Arizona where she was living at that time

Well how do you refuse an offer like that?   I didn't, I grabbed it with both hands, and in due course the tickets arrived. The excitement when the FEDEX man arrived at my door a few weeks later with these tickets. It was real I was going to the States for a holiday!

I set off at the end of August to fly to Boston. It was drizzle when at Glasgow Airport but this time it is a trip for fun with no worry. Being a person who is punctual I was early so sat and watched planes taking off. The domestic lounge was very quiet only three other people there when I arrived. The plane to London was called Delftblue Daybreak, which I thought was a lovely name. I had a rush to connect at London due to flight from Glasgow being late, and boarded without time to draw breath five minutes before doors close, no time to look through Duty Free. Thought I would ask my cousin if her travel agent knows how long it takes to transfer terminals at London. There was no leeway as it took half an hour to get off and get bus plus half an hour for plane being late, which meant getting to gate 21 was a sprint!

Later had fun filling in customs form as couldn't remember Andrea's address to start with, as forgot to bring that and her phone number. As there was an empty seat between me and the other passenger it made for a very comfortable flight.

At Logan International at Boston it was announced that we would sit for ten minutes, after 20 minutes they announced it was Irish minutes, flying Aer Lingus, very good sense of humour. Eventually we got into the building and got off the plane. Customs cleared very quickly and went through to be met by all three smiling faces and heard "There she is" as Skip took a photo of me walking and pulling my case.

I lost any tiredness and we after driving for about an hour we arrived at Judy's house at Buzzard's Bay, a lovely beach house where we stayed for the weekend, chatting and catching up in person as we hadn't seen each other for years, since they had visited Scotland.

Next morning got up early and went onto porch and see out over the Bay. It was very tranquil. Skip made pancakes for breakfast, what else in the USA. We were able to swim in the bay which was good, but had to wear beach shoes as it was a very sharp gritty beach.

That evening we went up and sat on the Widows Walk at the top of the house, this was reached by going through a trapdoor and up a ladder, but once up there the view was lovely. It is so called as when the fishermen were due in their wives would go to the top of the houses to watch for them, and inevitably when there were storms, some were left as widows.

After the weekend we relocated to Manchester, New Hampshire, and from that base spent a week, visiting various places, not least Boston, where after parking in a multi-storey carpark, we got the tube into the city. We walked a bit and saw the State House and The Black Memorial, which is very intricate and is at Boston Common. After that we walked up through the city to the Pannier Market and had a look round.

The next suggestion was that we did a trolley tour which we walked down a long wharf to get on board. What a great way to see the city as you can leave and re-join, a hop on hop off tour, we stayed on till we got to the USS Constitution (Old Ironsides) where a young sailor told us about the ship, which had been a British ship in the reign of George III we then re-joined the tour and got off at the Boston Tea Party site, where we got a snack, they eat a lot of ice cream, which I don't, so I bought crisps, they call chips, but the Irish girl from Belfast who was working on the Kiosk understood my accent. We then walked through the financial district and shopping areas to the Boston Common, then went to Cheers for a beer, before walking back through the gardens a bit and saw the "Make Way for Ducklings" statues which are enchanting. It is a lovely children's story. There is the mother duck followed by her ducklings which children sit on. Nancy Reagan asked the artist to reproduce them for Raisa Gorbachev so the only other place you can see them is in Red Square in Moscow. We walked back to the tube and went back to the car, and later had takeaway pizzas. The tiles inserted in the pavements let you follow the Freedom Trail in Boston.

Next day we set of for the Maine coast, and drove to Ogonguit Beach and parked the car, then got a tour trolley down to Perkins Cove for a look round this lovely village, which is a summer resort. Went into a shop specialising in ornamental lighthouses and pictures of them, and after buying two fridge magnets the lady insisted on giving me lighthouse earrings. We then got the trolley back up and went to the beach for a picnic which was leftover calzone from our takeaway the night before, and made a good picnic. We left there about 5.00pm and went down to Hampton, where we went to a seafood restaurant, fortunately there were prawn dishes, as unfortunately I am allergic to lobster. On the way home we saw the Nubble Lighthouse which is famous and featured in a lot of pictures.

A trip to Canterbury was arranged for me to see a preserved village which was run by the Shaker community. They had a schoolhouse and laundry, this was fascinating, they had drying racks which they loaded and then pushed into a warmed area, and left the clothes to dry, then could pull out the racks to unload them. Meanwhile that area was used for dealing with the previous dried laundry. Very efficient, but I found out the reason the community foundered was when the young people wanted to go out into the world, and there were not enough people left wanting that simple way of life. It was very interesting, to see how they had lived being self- sufficient, in many ways, like the Amish. Again an idea brought from another country. The next outing was to Weir's Beach on Lake Winnipasaukee and went on a boat called Mount Washington, for a sail round the lake which is huge.

There are numerous islands scattered all over the lake and seemingly when the lake freezes in winter people use sledges to take materials over to the islands, and that is how a lot of the houses on these islands got built. Of course in summer the materials would need to be shipped over. Some houses are exceptionally grand. I was told the lake is 72sq.miles in area.

The depth of the lake was given as between 180 and 200 feet in the commentary from the wheel-house and the trip lasted two and a half hours.

My relations were determined to show me as much of New England as they could and I also was meeting some of the family for the first time. One of these days was when we were going to Portsmouth New Hampshire. It was like stepping into a town in Devon, amazing feeling. This was a prime example of the emigres taking their way of life and architecture with them. The giveaway was the cars driving on the "wrong" side of the streets, and the double yellow lines up the middle of the road.

The next day I was taken to Exeter, where we had breakfast with my cousin's mother in law, afterwards we went on to Kensington and met up with the entire Sinclair family, at the home of one of my cousins. That was a tremendous reunion for I hadn't seen some of the cousins for years, and had just met one for the first time, a couple of days before. My elderly uncle was just enjoying being with his family, although his memory was bad and he kept asking me who I was.

That was the end of my week touring New England and at the weekend it was time to go back to South Dartmouth to Buzzard Bay and meet up again with my other cousin, and also meet her son and daughter. So another family party ensued, and a barbeque was on the go. After the weekend my cousin Andrea and her husband Skip who had been so good taking me everywhere had to go back to work. I found out then that our American cousins do not get as generous holiday allowances as was the norm at that time in the UK.

After they had left, Judy and I went and met a friend of hers for dinner, and when we came back to the house, I saw what I thought was a mouse lying on the decking. It was a tiny bat, it was only when I went to try to move it with a shovel, that it opened its wings and flew away. What a fright I got a flying mouse!

Two days later Judy and I flew to Phoenix and were met by a driver who took us to the house she was staying in at Sedona. I loved Sedona we did a trolley tour, and went up to a chapel in the rock which was lovely but we had to watch the heat as it was summer! It is very high very red rock and quite awesome to see, but when you go in it is quite dim after being in the brilliant sunlight.

After looking in the chapel we had to be sure to be outside in time for the next trolley as otherwise there would have been a lengthy wait, not to be recommended in these temperatures. Even in the chapel where it was cool, it would have been difficult to wait too long. I enjoyed the heat as it is a dry heat, no humidity.

We went to a restaurant every night, as Judy didn't do cooking, and spent quite a bit of time playing scrabble, but she always beat me. My spending money was lasting very well, as she would not let me pay for anything. I got the impression she enjoyed treating me as it was done so very kindly. The Arizona desert was absolutely stunning; as were some of the rock formations and we went to visit a couple who lived in the middle of nowhere, the man made kitchen cupboards out of recycled wood.

We were offered Margaritas with the salt round the rim, which we said yes to. While we were sipping a wasp was buzzing us, and Judy and her carpenter friend were discussing kitchen cabinets, while the wife and I were talking generally about Arizona, then the wasp dived into my drink, "Oh!" I said, as it landed in my drink, before I could do anything the glass was whipped out my hand and drink thrown away, while she said "Oh you can't drink that now". Did another replacement arrive?.....Em!... "no" I would have loved to have tasted that Margarita!

We set off one morning to go to the Grand Canyon, and in Flagstaff met with a friend of my cousin who was coming with us. As we were heading for the Hopi tribe reservation, there was a tremendous thunder storm on the way with the most spectacular fork lightning which was unlike anything I had ever seen. It had stopped just before we got to the Cameron Reservation and we were able to get out and go and look without getting wet. There was a gift shop there too, and I eventually was able to buy myself something. I got two little carved doll type ornaments, I had seen one which was gorgeous, and discovered it was the total amount I had for spending money, so settled for the affordable ones. I enjoyed looking at the lovely beadwork these people had made. Another interesting thing I had learned on the way there was that the Saguaro Cactus only grow up to a certain level as it becomes too cold. They can reach a height of 45 feet.

I was amazed at the depth of the Grand Canyon and the fact that the Colorado River, looked like a trickle from where we were above it. I know it is not a trickle but that shows the distance from the Rim to the valley floor.

After looking at the awe inspiring view of the Grand Canyon we went for lunch at a hotel which looked like a log cabin and had a fabulous meal, with the friends who had joined us.

The enormity of the Canyon, has to be seen, no way can it be described. I was very surprised to learn that at one time there was a covering of water on parts of Arizona as fossils of fish and other creatures have been found.

On the last day of my stay in Sedona, we had been to a vintage bridal fashion show, where some really old wedding dresses had been modelled, and we had tea and cakes. It was a charity fund raiser. Later after lunch we went to a Golf Club, where the Flagstaff Symphony Orchestra was giving a concert outside. We got ourselves seats where it was a bit shaded as the heat was intense, but it was interesting for me from the UK to be able to sit out and be sure it would be warm. We had a lovely afternoon, and as it started to darken the Cicadas started to click in the trees, and it became quite noticeable. That night we went for our final dinner, and I immediately after that had to leave as a car came to take me back to Phoenix. My flight the next day had been cancelled and the travel agent had got me on the red eye to Boston.

That in itself was interesting, as there I was all dressed in light summer clothes boarding a plane at Phoenix to fly north to a more temperate area. I tried to sleep but it was so cold on the plane, the airline staff were very casual, and as we were approaching Boston early in the morning, were distributing bottles of water, with an almost indifferent attitude, like toss and you catch it. I had travelled with my cousin southwards in first class, but economy was a totally different experience. The airline did have a nickname but I will refrain from using it. Not one of my favourite airlines!

Once back in Boston my generous cousin had booked me a room at the Novotel at the Harbour, so I could rest for the day as my flight to Scotland was not till evening, and was another overnighter, it was lovely looking over Boston harbour, but a bit misty. The hotel was very helpful, and most accommodating, and told me to keep the room till 5.00pm as I had only arrived in the morning. They arranged for the courtesy bus to take me to the airport. Once there I had ages to wait, but everything went to time, and before I knew it was back in the UK after an amazing holiday.

Chapter 8

Thank Goodness for Good Friends.

Shortly after that my Mum had floored me by announcing, that my Dad had decided he would like to see where it was she had been, when she took ill. Nothing daunted, they had booked to go the following January, 2001. I nearly had a bad turn, and thought this cannot be happening. Mum had only just got over her illness and it had taken fully 6 months for her to recover so we are at September 2000, when she announces she has something to tell me. They had got holiday insurance arranged, in my Mum's case at great expense, although Dad was older he was in exceptionally good health, and had not been hammered with huge excesses. This from the woman who could not walk unaided when I brought her home, and even six months later was not really mobile, had a stair-lift installed and was now telling me they were going back to see where she had been!

That Christmas Eve, my Dad had a stroke and was taken into hospital, and I must confess to being relieved, not that I was glad Dad was ill, just that their ambitions of a long haul holiday back to the scene of so much worry for me had been averted. Call it selfish if you like, but I had been faced with their plan of a repeat performance. Dad had made the remark "Oh I would like to see where you were so well cared for!" Well I think my feelings showed on my face OK they were old and maybe not realising they were old. As Rabbie Burns said, "Tae see oorsels as ithers see us" I am now glad to say my parents did not see themselves as old, Mum's illness in Argentina more of an inconvenience. But at 87 and 92 as they were, mentally they were still thinking 60 maybe 65 and 70's. Good on them, saving the pension and going to see the world. Do we not now wish we could in safety, now we are looking at that smaller part we can explore? My parents were inspirational!

However I digress I spent the following months enjoying my father's company, taking him for walks and getting him to talk about trips they had done, I have so many unidentified photos taken by him even yet. They had travelled so far and to places now unattainable. I was mesmerised. My father said to me whilst listening to a squirrel arguing with another in a tree, listen to all that is around you go and see the world and enjoy travelling. That was six months before he died. At this point my friends and I decided to go to a more formal Spanish class as well as the group we were involved with, and it proved beneficial although I was finding it hard to concentrate with Dad now being ill.

In 2002 in January, immediately after my father died, my girlfriends and I had a holiday to Lanzarote which was therapeutic for me, this had been booked some months earlier and my Dad had worried I wouldn't get, although everyone was saying I must go, but circumstances made it possible.

We were leaving the day after his funeral, and we had all booked fake tans, so at my dear old Dad's funeral there were a group of ladies decidedly tanned, even slightly orange, which at that time in January in Scotland was not common. Everyone knew we were going away, and many other friends said they would look out for Mum while I was off with my group.

This group of friends had been formed, when after my Argentine rescue mission, I had decided to learn Spanish, and had spoken to a man, who had done his Higher Spanish, a Scottish Secondary School qualification. Another lady in the church had also said to him, so we got our little group started, and this group of ladies met in September 2000 were the friends now getting me away for a holiday. They were keeping me busy each day going to see the sights, many of which I have described in an earlier chapter. One of my friends said to me let's do a Jeep Safari, so I agreed, it was great fun and took us to parts we wouldn't have found otherwise and was interesting as it got us into some more rural settings, it was very bumpy though and we were quite glad when we had a lunch stop, and free time.

We found a lovely wee restaurant in a fishing village and had a really lovely meal.

One night we had gone out for a Chinese Meal as there was a good restaurant relatively close to our apartments, the food was lovely and one of my friends dropped some sauce on her new top, leaving a nasty stain, panic stations as this was the start of the holiday. However from some depths of my brain I remembered reading that toothpaste was good for stain removal. So we plastered it on the top after we went back to our apartment, and next day rinsed it out and it worked! A tried and tested travel tip! Ok it was white toothpaste; don't know if it would work with the striped stuff!

There was a lovely pool at the apartments, and we spent some time in it, also tried to use Spanish but found the waiters wanted to practice English. We went all over the place and saw lots of things enjoyed the sunshine, and generally I felt it had helped me enormously. We went to Los Jameos Del Agua where there are volcanic galleries and caverns formed by a spectacular subterranean volcanic tube, probably started three or four thousand years ago. This centre was supervised by Cesar Manrique and has plants, pools and down in the dark in a pool there are white crabs, and is another example of the vision of Cesar Manrique.

When I got back home, Mum had been busy thinking, sensibly I may add this time, and had come up with a plan. The plan was that we would fly to Tenerife and join the Saga Rose for the last leg of her world cruise, four days sailing from there to Southampton. We would have a few days in a hotel first before joining the ship.

Cruising again!

This was all booked up by Mum who had decided that friends from Cornwall would come too so of we set first to Gatwick and an overnight stay and meeting up with Ann & John from Cornwall, family friends from way back. Mum had suggested that as two of my sons were working in London, they should come to the hotel for dinner if at all possible, so they joined us to Grandma's delight, and a very merry dinner was had. Next day we flew to Tenerife and had a four night stay in a lovely hotel, and I could try out the little Spanish I had by then learned, and was relatively successful. On arrival they had allocated us a double room when we had asked for twin, so as the receptionist didn't speak English and the Saga rep didn't speak Spanish, I with my trusty dictionary did my best. We got a lovely twin room with a small balcony, and the extra pillows Mum needed. One night in the restaurant at the hotel I remarked that I loved patatas canarian, and the next night from the kitchen a large platter was brought out to our table. The lovely patatas, they are cooked with sea salt coating the outside. There were so many after we had taken our share they were passed around the rest of the Saga group awaiting the ship. I am sure it was because I asked in Spanish!

Mum wanted to see the tropical garden where she and Dad had visited so the four of us set of and slowly in stages got there and had a lovely morning looking at the beautiful plants; some of the trees were interesting too as species not seen in Scotland.

I particularly liked the orchid house and would have spent longer there, but we had to get Mum back to the hotel for a rest and then Ann, John and I set off to explore further along the town of Puerto de la Cruz, and found a café where we had a lovely lunch. We were sitting looking out over a little harbour, where people were swimming, a tranquil setting.

We could look back and see the Hotel we were staying in, as it was built into the side of the cliff.

We also noticed a lot of the living statues who, when you went to photograph them pointed to their collection pots!

Great excitement four days later when it was time to join the ship at Santa Cruz, which we did in time for lunch, as the passengers already sailing with her, had mainly gone on trips, We had a lovely twin cabin, and Ann & John were quite near in their cabin. We had a lovely time, Ann and Mum sat together a lot, and John liked to sunbathe and I like to sit and watch the sea, so everyone had something they enjoyed.

We of course had the Captain's cocktail party which was a lovely reason to get dressed up as it was the final formal night. Captain Warden-Owen was lovely and Mum loved us getting a photograph with the Captain.

I was about the youngest apart from one other daughter travelling with her Mum, but it became evident she had her own agenda, she was ostensibly travelling with Mum but obviously had set up an assignation, although married and travelling with her Mum she was frequently seen in a very close situation with a gentleman, who was not her husband as she said he was in Hampshire travelling to work, it transpired she was a regular passenger with her mother who did not like to travel alone. How convenient! It was a lovely ship, not too big a ship to negotiate with an elderly lady, very good entertainment, and the food was excellent. She was originally a Cunard ship and obviously had retained the style when taken over by Saga. They did the white glove afternoon tea, and chef's parade with the Bombe Alaska. Too soon our sea days were over and time to disembark at the QE2 terminal, Southampton.

Chapter 9

The QE 2 is calling!

Early in 2003, I saw an article in a newspaper, about the QE2 going to do a Tandem Crossing with QM2 from New York to Southampton; this was mentioned as being in April 2004 and would be her final voyage as flagship. A friend, who was a widow, had sailed previously on a few occasions with her late husband on the ship.

So as I visited her regularly I broached the subject of would she be interested, did she feel she could do this, as doing it with someone else could be difficult. However, she said yes she would, and we started planning. She was keen on staying at the Waldorf Astoria, so having phoned Cunard and asked to be preregistered for this voyage which was not yet on sale, I got onto the internet and started investigating prices for the Waldorf thinking it would be out of our budget.

Very shortly after this we got a phone call from Cunard which was to tell us we had a cabin, so I then booked directly with the Waldorf and got the good deal I had seen, as it was so far ahead. Next move was to decide what sights we wanted to see and what show to go and see. Empire State building was selected and 42nd Street, so I got them booked direct as well. Hadn't occurred to me to use a travel agent as at that time we didn't have one in our village.

Next we had to organise our wardrobes, so that was an excuse to visit a relatively new Bridal Shop in the village which also was doing Prom dresses and evening gowns, so trying on was done, and colours decided on, and orders placed. We then had to check we had suitably glamourous shoes and evening bags. Budget forgotten, we were not going to stint ourselves!

QE2 and QM2, Tandem Crossing 2004.   New York to
Southampton

Finally the day came when we flew from Glasgow to
London Heathrow and when getting our passes checked
were told we were getting upgraded for the flight to New
York, business class with BA well we were thrilled as
were two other ladies boarding, also going to have a
short holiday in the city.

 We couldn't believe our luck.   We were treated like
royalty; the cabin had the new style seats which if you
wished you could flatten to sleep in. We were in the
centre of the cabin so our seats were side by side,
however, there was an American couple off to my left,
and the woman kept complaining as their seats were
side by side but facing in opposite directions, unlike ours
both facing same way, her husband kept telling her to be
quiet, but to no avail. Eventually having ordered our
meal, when it came the stewards who by this time knew
we were on a special trip had asked which wine we
would like, and when they said they only had one bottle

left of it, the other steward, said no it was OK she had another in her galley. So wine was produced poured into a proper glass, and just as I was taking my first forkful of my meal, my glass received a direct hit from a chocolate and the wine went over me, I buzzed for the stewardess, and handing her the chocolate said I believe this belongs to that woman over there and I am covered in wine as it hit my glass! I was mopped up and even damp cloths were brought to stop my clothes from staining from the red wine.

We got a bit mixed up filling in the immigration cards which was partly down to the fact my friend doesn't do forms, so I was doing hers as well as my own, and the fact we had been well "treated" in more ways than one. Eventually I had it done and the purser checked them, but he didn't tell me I hadn't filled in both sides which I had to do in a hurry once we were in the queue for passport control in the airport, thanks to another couple pointing this out. This possibly was due to the fact he couldn't stop laughing as I kept saying nope got it wrong again, can I please have another two cards.

As we were leaving the plane, both he and the stewardess, came and said how much they had enjoyed hearing about our plans' and as a present here was the last bottle of the wine, for us to take to the hotel. I then asked about the couple of chocolate fame who had vanished, and was told they had been escorted off first for causing a disturbance!

My niece's husband ran a limousine business so he collected us and took us to the hotel, and we said we would want him to come back and take us to the ship in three days' time. So we said we would phone with times later.

We got into the hotel, went wow at the chandelier as we entered and the gorgeous flower arrangement and then as we walked onto the carpet in the lobby your feet just sank into it, such luxury. I had booked for zip check-in, and as we were in a queue, a receptionist came up and asked if she could help, so I said, where do we go for zip-check-in, we were promptly taken to a side room, sat down and checked in. A porter then took our cases and we were escorted to the lifts and taken to our room. Lovely old fashioned furniture and two enormous queen size beds! Bliss a coffee machine. We were only taking out what we needed for our New York adventure, so shortly after went to find somewhere to eat, and were joined by my cousin's daughter for a meal, I was shattered and could hardly stay awake with the time difference.

Next morning we went to Oscar's restaurant in the hotel for breakfast, and our waiter who was Egyptian told us how to get to the Empire State Building and also told us to later go on the Staten Island ferry as it was free! We had our tickets for 11.00am for the Empire State Building so off we went and had a good look at that and while up at the observation deck saw QM2 going off from her berth with some corporate people who were being shown her. QE2 was still on her way across the Atlantic to join us. It was amazing seeing the size of the ship even from that height.

When we came back out on to Fifth Avenue, we had decided we were not doing shopping, no definitely no we would go and get coffee and a sandwich or something like that. We found a café and had our snack, and then thought we would go back to the hotel and get a cab to the ferry. However, there was a shoe shop, and it had a sign in the window saying SALE, how could we resist? We couldn't and didn't, four pairs of shoes later we emerged back onto the street, and said well we have to go back and drop off our purchases, then we will do the ferry.

We did the trip to Staten Island in the afternoon and it was very interesting, our waiter had said we could stay on, but as there was increased security because of 9/11 we had to be counted off and walk round to another gate and re-board, but that wasn't a problem, the views from the ferry of the skyline and the Statue of Liberty were great, but we didn't have enough time to see Liberty as well.

That night we stayed in the hotel and just had a good look at the shops in it, and again were tempted to buy ourselves nice things, plus getting something to eat and having a few drinks. We then retired to our room to get ready for bed and read for a wee while, so we would be fresh for Central Park the next day. Later that evening in our room, the telephone rang to our surprise, and it was my old school friend Garth who I had stayed with in Canada, so we had a great chat!

We had planned on having a carriage ride through the park but when we got there and spoke to the drivers, the only option was a ride round outside the park as there was a march on! Nothing daunted we decided that would be OK, and very pleasant it was going round the streets and our knowledgeable driver pointing out various famous buildings. As we passed the Jimmy Choo shop a lot of the staff waved to us, must have recognised shoe lovers, although they were beyond our budget!

When we returned to the start point we had our photo taken with the horse called Major, and gave him carrots as a reward. We then decided we could walk through part of the park and had a good amble before going a couple of blocks back to the hotel.

That evening after dinner, we got the doorman to hail a stretch limo to take us to the Ford Theatre to see 42nd Street, we had agreed a price with the guy but at one point he stopped and these other women got in, a few blocks later he stopped and they got out, so we felt we had been duped, as we still had to pay the price agreed. After the theatre show which was fabulous, we danced along the street a little way, and found another stretch limo and driver, and told him we wanted it to ourselves and he was not to pick up anyone else as we had been conned earlier. We arrived back at the Waldorf feeling like a couple of Duchesses.

It had by now been arranged with Catriona my niece's husband that he would drop her off with the kids, and take another couple to the port, come back and get us and give us a tour

He was as good as his word, and we had an hour with the family, before all going in the car for a tour, he got us to Wall Street, told us to jump out as not allowed to park up and we went and got our photo taken with the Bull, the symbol of Wall Street, and jumped back in further down the street. I understand that no cars are allowed to even stop temporarily now. We were shown us the Cunard building, and he circled while we did a quick tour of Grand Central Station, a sombre look at Ground Zero, which I found so sad, and the quietness of it, not a bird chirping. All the photos still up on the fences; it was a heart wrenching experience.

Catriona and John then took us to a Jewish deli, on 2nd Street, which was very famous, and we had a lovely lunch. I understand that members of the same family still operate a deli but it is in a different locale of New York now.

The sandwiches were ordered, and when they came it was to us Brits, a yard of sandwiches, huge. We womanfully did our best to consume our order. Their boys loved it, once we had finished up, we thanked John for his generosity, as we were paying him, or so we thought, to take us to the ship. We had to put the money in his shirt pocket and tell him he had to keep it for the boys if nothing else.

All the way to the port he kept up a commentary about where we were and what this and that building were.

We had lots of hugs and kisses, and said our farewells, and got on with the business of boarding the QE2 for this historic crossing of the Atlantic.

Once we were in our cabin, the champagne was opened and we had a chat about whether or not to unpack, the consensus was no that could wait a while, so we sipped and then eventually got ourselves partly unpacked, then headed for the lifeboat drill session. Once that was over, we decided that perhaps refreshment was on the cards, so not ones to hold back we headed for the nearest bar, which was in the Chart Room, with the lovely map of the World behind the bar and the moving QE2 on it as we progressed on our voyage. Obviously at that point it was firmly showing as being in New York!

Only then did we return to finish unpacking, and then headed off for dinner, as later that evening, we were having a late departure as there were going to be fireworks. We were informed that this was the first firework display in New York since the tragedy of 9/11.

The two ships left the quaysides within fifteen minutes of each other easing out into the Hudson River, with crowds on the quayside and all around, bands playing, flags waving, those of us on board waving flags of our home nations, the ships adjacent to each other. Passengers on both ships were served champagne during the half hour of the display and a myriad of small boats and river cruise boats with passengers all enjoying this spectacle. We then halted in the middle of the river with one ship slightly ahead as the fireworks started to go up from barges in the river, in the area around the Statue of Liberty, she was illuminated by floodlights and the whole scenario was breath-taking, the cameras could be seen as the passengers of both ships recorded the event. Spine tingling, I was taking video, and by the end of it my fingers were numb. As the display came to an end both ships sounded their horns, the QM2 sounded first followed by QE2, with both ships and the New York skyline lit up it was a brilliant sight.

The following four nights were formal nights with the Masters of both ships, Captain McNaught of the QE2 and Commodore Warwick of the QM2, hosting various cocktails parties for the passengers who were all given a commemorative passenger list, certificate and inscribed plate. The ships photographers in situ each evening to capture this momentous occasion, and on Monday 26th April both ships held Gala Dinners. At night it was lovely to see the QM2 all lit up and sailing along and each night flashes from each ship as we took photos of the other one.

Having had a pretty smooth crossing apart from one day and evening, and able to get outside most days, Friday 30th April at 2.30pm, was another amazing experience, as having sailed across one mile apart during the day, the ships changing sides each night, they were sailing much closer going past the Lizard as there was a flypast with a Hawk and Nimrod of the RAF this all being photographed from a helicopter.

The planes first flew upper deck level along the starboard side of the QE2 flew off in a circle, came back flew in front of the QM2 and circled again and flew between the ships, turned and flew back between them again. The decks were packed with passengers on both the ships, and you could see the passengers on the other ship although they looked very small.

After this Captain McNaught announced that this was the end of the display and as the two ships drew level the horn of the QM2 sounded three times, to which the QE2 on giving the first of the answering blasts, every passenger on deck cheered, and continued cheering as

113

the grand old lady gave another two mighty blasts.

There was to be a special photo opportunity on the 30th April as passengers on the QE2 were able to be photographed beside the Boston Cup, which was presented by the city of Boston to Samuel Cunard in 1840 in recognition of him sailing his ships from Liverpool to Boston and not New York. This was being handed over from QE2 on the afternoon of the 1st May to Commodore Warwick Master of the QM2 as the new flagship of the Cunard Line.

QE2 last night as flagship, and sad at our trip being at an end. The next morning we actually went for breakfast and met our one table companion who had never come for dinner, as being alone at breakfast didn't realise he could have had company for dinner.

However, a pleasant couple of hours were spent waiting to disembark, now that the adventure was over.

She is the longest serving Cunard liner, she sailed out of Southampton on 2nd May 2004 for a refit 35 years to the day from her maiden voyage, and she is STILL the fastest.

Chapter 10

Return to Argentina.

Thanks to my friends who had gone with me on holiday in 2002, I had enjoyed other Canary Island holidays with them going to Tenerife as well as Lanzarote, Mum had been needing looked after so, going exciting places had been on hold, and short holidays were the order of the day. However Mum had died in 2005, and after moving house and sorting all such matters out, in 2006 I saw a trip advertised to Argentina, with Titan Tours, and thought how wonderful it would be to go back and find Louis Alberto whom I had been in touch with but with email addresses changing and my lack of Spanish, contact had been lost, although I was still in touch with Bettina who had been a waitress at the Hotel del Glacier. She was now living in the USA.

Got the brochure, studied it and this trip covered from Buenos Aires up to Iguazu Falls, back to BA, and to several other places including Ushuaia, Tierra del Fuego.

Perfect! I phoned them up and spoke to a very helpful person, and booked it there and then. I would fly from Glasgow to Gatwick where I would meet with the rest of the group the following October, 2007.

The flight from Glasgow was fine, and on arriving at Gatwick made my way to the meeting point which I found without any difficulty. There was a good sized group probably about 25 of us, including Penny from Edinburgh, who was our group guide who would liaise with the local guides as she spoke fluent Spanish. We were duly ticked off the list, and made our way to board the first flight which was to Madrid, where we were changing planes. From Madrid I had booked an upgrade, as being totally aware of the length of this leg of the journey and wanted space. We boarded and it was lovely turning left, and being shown to my seat, there was another lady in the window seat, so after saying hello, and introducing ourselves, it transpired she was a fellow passenger on the same trip. She was also travelling alone, so was quite happy to chat and pass the time. Later as it was night we managed to get to sleep, as we both knew it would be a long day the next day.

The arrival at Buenos Aires went very smoothly and we were ushered onto lovely tour coaches for our trip into the city from Ezezia Airport, and were given a tour en-route, as we now also had a local guide, who was called Maria Irma. This was a very detailed tour, and she was very informative. The first glimpse was of the Jacaranda Trees, with their lovely blossoms, a very impressive city, with many fine buildings. I had noticed on the way in from the airport, the shanty town I had seen seven years previously, and as the guide said when passing it, they were just building up higher, still with the electric wires hanging outside the buildings and draped in loops, and although the railway company wanted them gone to be able to extend the railway the fact they had been there a long time was making it difficult for the government. We were taken to La Boca, and given some time to look around, and get a coffee. I did just that, and loved the colourful houses. This is not an area to go to at night, as it is quite near the docks we were told. There were people dancing tango in the street, our introduction to tango, we just watched although some people were being encouraged to try. Indeed we had discovered that later at the hotel a couple would join our group, as they had come earlier to have tango lessons.

We then were taken to a restaurant for lunch; the entrance to the restaurant had a model of a cow just at the door, which indicated it was a steak restaurant. The food was wonderful; we were made to feel so welcome.

We arrived at our hotel early afternoon, and in a lovely little lounge area in Hotel de las Americas, were able to get coffee and sandwiches, for Mary and myself. At this point Penny was telling us about a trip to a ranch which was available the next day so we paid our $76 for this trip. We then went to our rooms and agreed to meet later, it was interesting how to work the lights, as the key card for the door had to be inserted in a slot inside the room, but as this was also your entry key, it caused some hilarity to those who like us only had one! We had also noticed that the staff didn't all speak English although English was more noticeable than it had been seven years previously.

Next day, after breakfast we were meeting in the foyer joining the group for the trip to the Santa Susanna Ranch. A mini bus took us there with Penny and our local guide, Maria Irma, who was excellent, the drive out to the ranch was interesting and one building which was quite grand turned out to be the water treatment plant.

We were greeted at the ranch by a very colourful Gaucho, and our local guide explained that the belt he wore covered in silver coins called a Rastra. He and Maria Irma both liked drinking Mate a type of tea from their mate pots made from gourds. Sometimes plain but also can be elaborately decorated.

We were pointed in the direction of the original ranch house with all its old furnishings, and is now a museum, and showed how early life on the ranch was. Later we were all to meet for lunch in a huge barn where the gauchos would serve us. Just before that we were also given the opportunity to go horse riding or have a ride in a wagon, which was up and down a field, which was the option I took, and very interesting it was, as our gaucho who didn't speak much English pointed out birds like ground owls, and one of our companions was knowledgeable about birds and could tell us the names. We also saw lapwings including a baby one.

The family who run the ranch now live in a larger more modern house, and breed horses.

The dining room table in the museum house was huge and everywhere in the house there were display cases and frames including a most wonderful collection of fans.

The sides of lamb were hung at an angle from tripods over wood fires outside, to barbeque them, there were long tables set for us, bowls of salad and potatoes, and then we were given the choice of beef, lamb or chicken for our meat or a mixture of those. The wine was poured, excellent Argentine wines, including Malbec from Mendoza, their famed wine growing area. After the main course was served, there was an entertainment of a couple dancing tango on a small stage accompanied by a guitar, and Nandeo which is a small type of accordion used in playing tango music. There also was someone singing traditional very haunting songs.

Then we were served various postres, as they love their sugary cakes and puddings.

After the meal and entertainment we had been supposed to go outside to see some gaucho's throwing bolas, and other horseback activities, however a thunderstorm had started, and the barn and houses had no gutters, so it was amazing to see this torrential rain pouring off the roofs straight down. Several of the gauchos had disappeared, and shortly after it became apparent why, as they had gone out to bring the horses in. We stood at the windows and watched as they galloped in with a herd of horses, one in particular caught our eye as the mare kept herself between the gaucho's horse and her foal, the little foal kept up very well, but it was lovely to see the mare protecting her youngster! The gauchos were dressed in very long waterproof capes, so their colourful dress was well covered up. We then went through to the little gift shop and got a few souvenirs. My little hand carved gaucho stands on my sideboard, with his bolas, ready for action.

We were then sheltered by umbrellas as we got back into the minibus to go back to the hotel. By this time we had got to know the names of most of our group, where they were from, and some of them had travelled a lot, but for two of us it was a return to Argentina. The other lady had worked on a ranch with horses previously and had driven from the USA on the Pan American highway right down to Tierra del Fuego many years ago, working as she went. She was now travelling with her mother. I spent a good lot of time over the next two weeks in their company.

When we got back to the hotel, Lesley, Mary and I had coffee, before Lesley went off to join her mother. Mary and I decided a bowl of soup would keep us going instead of another meal.

The next day I worked out how to change the pins on my travel plug so I could charge up my camcorder. I didn't realise that two of them could be slanted and that was the required format for Argentina. We had a wander round the streets near to the hotel, but generally just spent a quiet day as were heading for Iguazu the next day.

Up bright and early for breakfast then everyone gathered to go to the airport to fly to Iguazu. Now at this time of year in Buenos Aires, the temperature was quite pleasant, little did we realise how hot it was in Iguazu. The travel instructions had said to bring a hat! This particular brain of Britain had brought a sun visor; however as soon as we got off the plane on the tarmac at Iguazu, I knew a hat was going to be a must! While on the plane I had got chatting to a couple from Barcelona, who had asked where in Scotland I was from as they had been to Ardrossan, for the ferry to the Island of Arran, five miles from where I live, we had a good laugh about that. It's a small world indeed!

It was only a ten minute bus ride to the hotel which was the Sheraton, which as it was so humid and hot was a blessing. The Sheraton, the last word in luxury, is the only hotel in the Rainforest in Argentina, and its setting is stunning. From reception you can see the mist rising from the falls, and from the lounge and terrace, and to the other side the rooms are looking onto the jungle, you hear the monkeys chattering, see all sorts of exotic birds, including toucans! There is a sign in the rooms saying to keep the sliding doors to balconies shut to keep out the monkeys! If that doesn't tell you it's a jungle out there nothing will! I was on the jungle side.

After our rooms were allocated and luggage deposited, a quick freshen up, and a walk with our guide to where the original Sheraton Hotel was, it is now a café/restaurant, so we could get some lunch. After lunch we had a walk across a very long metal bridge over the Iguazu River to the falls at a point called the Devil's Throat.

The view of the falls is breath-taking, and as there was a photographer there, those of us who had managed to get that far had a group photo taken. Some of the group had to turn back as they were being overcome by the heat. I had by this time bought a hat at a little stall near where we had lunch as I could feel the heat beating on the top of my head, and I have a good head of hair! Once we were back at the hotel, I had yet another shower and washed my hair, as it was so sticky.

While we were walking we saw a Cayman and a turtle in the river, and could see the colourful birds darting through the canopy of the trees. There was a banana tree with fruit outside the entrance to the hotel, and beautiful tropical flowers. The flowers lower down on the banana tree were bell shaped and a burgundy colour. The next morning as it gets light so early I was out on my balcony at 7.30 watching the birds, then went for breakfast which had bucks fizz with it as Sunday, seemingly a tradition at the hotel. After breakfast some people were going over to the Brazilian side, but I had opted to stay put and do the high walk first and get some video. Then I returned to my room, to have another shower, and change my sandals. The second walk I did the lower one and as there was a forest warden walking with us, he pointed out a huge iguana, and also stamped his feet to chase away a Coati which is a type of racoon like animal which bite. They are famed for eating coffee beans which are eventually once through them, their droppings are processed into some very expensive coffee, can't say I fancy that!

The filming did come out OK but like all overcome with the stunning scenery I had taken pictures of a lot of water! The temperature cooled a little in the afternoon, and some people went for a swim, in the hotel pool, as the forecast was for a storm. Some of us were quite looking forward to this as we thought it could be spectacular, but it turned out to be a little shower, the storm went elsewhere!

Went with another lady to the little café in the forest for a sandwich and water, as hot drinks were not what we needed. The hotel took down all the flags in case the wind got up to storm force.

We are now at the end of October, and I woke at 5.30 and went out to see what birds were around as they disappear as it heats up. I couldn't believe my eyes as there in front of me were three toucans. I didn't want to move in case I scared them away. Took some pictures, and sat quietly.

Shortly after when they had flown away, I finished packing my case, and went for breakfast, before the bus would come for us. Someone somewhere got the arrangements a bit wrong as they sent a tiny minibus for all of us and luggage. However another bus was summoned and duly arrived and we got to the airport in time.

Once back in Buenos Aires, it was Jorge Newberry airport for us, I could remember it so clearly, and I had the advantage as I knew where things were, so became the go to person for various reasons. At this point my hand luggage, which had been my Dad's, decided to collapse and my possessions were all over the floor. I asked Mary if she would mind if we went to the luggage shop to see what I could get, and off we trotted. I got a very nice red Samsonite spinner, paid for it and loaded my belongings into it. An expensive souvenir maybe, but it still serves me well. Ironic, I thought, that seven years after going through there, to get to Mum a bag belonging to my late Dad should collapse. We flew from there to Trelew for Puerto Madryn, which is a seaside town, and stayed in a lovely small hotel, Hotel Peninsula Valdes, it was small and comfortable, and very central to the town with some good restaurants nearby some of us tried out. It was by now getting cooler as we were moving south so warmer clothes were brought out of the case.

Lesley and I went for a walk and had a coffee, then found a camera shop as couldn't get camcorder to work, turned out the clear disc in the pack had stuck to the one I was trying to record to. That sorted we returned to the

Hotel. While having the coffee we met a family from Buenos Aires, so I got the chance to practise my Spanish and as Lesley spoke some Spanish as well, we had fun.

The next day we were taken on a whale watching trip, in quite a small boat. This little boat when stopped to watch a Southern Right whale and her calf, pitched a bit, and some of the other passengers were a strange colour. Fortunately I managed to do a little bit of filming on my phone while holding on with one hand, but not ideal, so no picture to prove it. After we came ashore we were taken to a ranch for a buffet lunch and loads of salad, this trip is being so well organised. Later we took a walk to a path at the cliff to look down onto a protected beach where there were elephant seals and one particular bull elephant seal was lying on his side flicking the gravel over his body, just like the David Attenborough programmes we had seen. This was too far to make a photograph possible, as we were on top of a cliff looking down.

We also saw Sea lions, and three penguins. On the way back from there we saw flamingos, and armadillo, and rhea. We had been provided with sheets with wildlife listed and had been told to shout out when we saw any and if possible the driver would stop to let photos be taken. We just caught sight of a fox as it was almost the same colour as the earth. As the roads are long fairly straight and miles from anywhere, there is very little traffic, so it is not a problem to stop. Also on the wheels of the coaches and heavy vehicles there is a special valve fitted so that if you are unfortunate enough to get a puncture, the wheel re-inflates till you get to a destination. Also if you come across anyone broken down, no matter what your vehicle is you stop and try to help. There everyone carries toolkits.

Next day we were off to Punto Tombo, a penguin rookery, where they dig burrows to lay their eggs, these are Magellan penguins, and we were able to walk along paths seeing hundreds of them, Dad often sitting on the eggs. Somehow or other I upset my camera bag, and lost a memory card with my photos from Iguazu, however several of my companions later posted me copies of theirs.

The penguins have burrowed into the earth but another favourite place is under the scrubby bushes where they are a bit disguised.

We were taken to Gaiman famous for being the town the Welsh settled, and went to a Tea Room for a Welsh tea, which means lots and lots of cakes. Beautiful home baking and cups of tea. It was very attractive driving through the Chubut valley on our way there, as after the pampas, it was really lush and fertile by comparison. We were told how when the Welsh arrived they had started off living in caves, and then had moved inland and even now in that area Welsh is spoken. At that time Tegwin Roberts was still alive, and although in her 80's still looking after the local museum.

On the way back we saw Caracara a falcon type of bird, Mara, a hare-like animal, Merino sheep, Guanacos which are animals like llamas, still marking them off the sheet we had.

Next stop Ushuaia, and hopefully my mission will come to fruition to find and thank Luis Alberto.

At the Trelew Airport initially our flight was to be delayed one hour, so when they called some of us to go to departures, we trotted off dutifully. Aha, then the problem arose, it was announced it would be another hour. Now some of us had snacks with us but others not, and we are now in a fairly small room, with a lot of other people, many of whom are nothing to do with our group, Penny our guide is still out on the other side of security, and my fellow companions are saying how can we get water or biscuits to keep us going. My Spanish may not have been very good at this point but was one hundred percent better than seven years previously, so I approached the security man and tried to say we needed water and biscuits and could I please be allowed to go back and buy some. I got out went to where the others were, made the purchases, and then tried to find the door I had gone through originally for security. It could not be seen. Wandered up and down this corridor a bit, until what seemed like an hour later, a man spoke and I tried again to explain I had been in departure lounge but had come out and now needed to take water to my friends! He opened the wall and there I was back in. Surreal, but after distributing the water and biscuits, we settled down for the duration. It was also quite funny as the luggage was being taken out to the plane, it passed where we were sitting and we were saying well they have my case, can you see yours?

Eventually we got boarded and settled down as it is a four hour flight to Ushuaia. When we arrived and got to the Hotel Ushuaia, I was so excited I couldn't settle and it was 1.00am, several of my fellow travellers had problems like they needed a bathplug or whatever, so once they were sorted out, I asked the man on the reception desk if by any chance he knew Luis Alberto

Lazo who had been a taxi driver in 2000. I had brought a photo with me of Luis Alberto and my Mum taken when we were at the airport to go home in 2000. He said yes, he was a friend of his and lives close to the hotel. So I asked him if he could tell him I was at the hotel, I then went for a drink with Penny and again thanked her for her support, as this bit of my trip was going to be very emotional.

I went to bed in my huge room, as I had a bedroom area with a huge sitting-room, as well as the en-suite facilities. Another single lady had the same. It seemed to be if you had paid the single person supplement you got a larger room, as this had happened in a few places where rooms came in different formats. This being an older hotel that was the case, it wasn't an all modern rooms type of hotel. It looked quite like a Swiss Chalet from the outside, and was right up at the back of Ushuaia at the opposite end from the Glacier Marcial.

On my way to breakfast later that same morning, I met the receptionist man, who patted me on the shoulder and said in Spanish that Luis would be there that evening. In the meantime my young friend Bettina had sent me the telephone number for her aunt and uncle, so nothing ventured I phoned the number and in my best Spanish asked them to come to the hotel and meet me that evening.

After breakfast Mary and I went shopping, I wanted a new fleece as the one bought seven years before was needing replaced. I found the shop again, and we also bought some T-shirts as souvenirs.

We then went on a trip to the National Park and went on the little train, the most southerly in the world; from the train we saw a grey fox. It was very cold where we had a stop, and we went back and sat on the train after taking photos. Once back at the main station, we re-boarded our coach and were taken to the Tolkyen Hotel for lunch, more chicken, lamb, beef empanadas, which are like mini pasties, and we saw Ibis, black rabbits, water rats, more upland geese and caracara, and grebe. After lunch we then went to Lapataia which is a lake and river going out to sea. I was frozen as had not used the new fleece but a lightweight rain jacket. On the way back to the hotel in Ushuaia our local guide had pointed out the hospital area, and said that one lady was on the bus whose mother had been in hospital there. I got a bit choked up at that, I had told her I had been in Ushuaia before and why, but hadn't expected her to mention it.

Once back at the Hotel in Ushuaia soon warmed up and we went to the restaurant for dinner. While eating Mary said to me I think that might be your friend coming, as I was fighting with a piece of fish full of bones, I looked up and there was my friend. I got up from the table and went and gave him a big hug as I was so pleased to see him. I introduced him to Mary, and explained she didn't speak any Spanish, and he insisted we finish our meal. I couldn't I was too excited at seeing him again after all this time.

We then went to the lounge in the hotel and en-route I saw Penny and asked if she would join us please as she was fluent in Spanish. I didn't realise the poor woman had not yet eaten. Give her all credit, she did and ate several hours later, after being with us by which time Carmen and Jose, Bettina's aunt and uncle had also joined us.

Luis Alberto left as he was working the next day. It was quite a reunion, and Penny was able to tell him in better detail how much his friendship had meant, as without it seven years earlier I would have had huge problems.

Luis Alberto had brought me a tango shawl his mother had crocheted. I had brought him a tartan scarf my mother had bought for him, before she died.

I was so happy to see him and to hear that he had remarried as he was a widower first time we met him.

As they left others of our group had witnessed the reunion and all said how happy they were for me. Lesley and her Mum had come in time to meet Louis Alberto and Jose and Carmen, and Penny said she had not been

138

expecting to be included but had felt privileged to be part of a very special occasion.

The next morning Penny said she had seen Luis heading for his work, which now was a Captain on one of the huge Catamarans which do the trips up the Beagle Channel and to other places. He was going on a five day trip. When we got to the dock, it was the Elizabetta our party was going on. It was a very wet day, but still able to see the Faro, the lighthouse which is famous.

We had a very good commentary in English while sailing up the Channel, and during our two hours on board, we saw Sea lions, Cormorants, and Antarctic Widgeon and Steamer Ducks which are flightless and we were all given a certificate to prove we had done it.

Coming back into Ushuaia the rain had eased and the view into the Bay and the town was pretty good. It was interesting to see it from the sea. Mary and I had a walk for an hour and a half with another couple and got pizza at a café, before we had to get ourselves organised to go to the Airport for the next destination which was El Calafate to see the Glaciers.

The Airport at Ushuaia is a modern bright airport, although due to the snow starting it meant our flight was late coming in. This is their spring time, but like our winter, and eventually we left and several hours later arrived in El Calafate. The hotel we were in this time, didn't have a restaurant of its own, so we had to go to the one next door, but didn't actually have to step outside to do this, and would get breakfast and dinner there.

Next morning, 2nd November, we left the hotel at 8am for Lago Argentina, we saw Condors flying, and black faced Ibis and another grey fox. Several people told us we had been so lucky to see so many Condors! We stopped at a viewpoint to take photos of Perito Moreno glacier, which is spectacular; there were calafate bushes and the calafate berries of the legend. Eat one and you will always come back to Argentina. We were told that the wind always blows from the west which lifts to pass over the mountains which irrigates the Andes. The wind stops at night when the ground is warmer, which is why the glacier is still there.

The first boat we were supposed to be getting couldn't sail as the wind had blown the ice across the wharf. Another boat was enquired about but it was fully booked, so we were being taken back to Calafate and had a walk round the town, and a look in the shops. Later we went for a meal in the restaurant which we thought was part of the hotel, and which was very good.

On the morning of the 3rd November we were taken to Puerto Bandera and got on the most beautiful catamaran, we were in superior salon, with leather seats, enormous windows, and again a very good commentary. We were sailing through icebergs, some of the colours were amazing, shades of blue and turquoise, and the shapes were varied. The main thing was not what we could see but the explanation of how far under the water they were. As we went up the Lake we saw the Agassi, Speggazini, and Upsala glaciers, the colours of these are in shades of aquamarine, white and even purple when the light hits a certain way. We even saw a glacier calving with an enormous splash, and could hear it creaking as it moved.

We then had some time ashore and there were local guides who could explain about the movement of the ice, and how there were huge rocks which had been brought to there on the force of the glaciers moving them, known as erratics. There were also trees that only grow there and wild cows which had been left when people had to move on as life was too hard. They are now trying to catch these animals as their bloodlines are so pure and they have very lean meat, and breed them with the ranch cattle. The glaciers reach across to Chile. We also saw woodpeckers, and one of the men in our group tried tapping a tree, and then heard a woodpecker answering by pecking whatever tree it was at.

When we got back we went for a walk again and then joined the same couple for dinner again in the restaurant, after we had ordered we sat, and sat, and sat. We saw other people coming in to the restaurant and being served, and eating finishing and going away. So eventually I got the attention of the waiter and tried in Spanish to ask him to send the boss, who was standing over at the bar. Nothing happened. I got up and went over to him and explained I only spoke a little Spanish did he speak English, the answer was no, so I tried to say it was now two and a half hours since we had ordered our meal, he shrugged! I gave up went back and sat down, and fifteen minutes later our food arrived, one of the meals was wrong so the husband of the lady with the wrong meal swapped with her. It was not even a good meal, but in a strange place at that timeof night what else could we do. When we went back to the Hotel, I spoke to the receptionist and said how bad it was, which was when I discovered it did not belong to the Hotel. Our companions said they would Trip Advisor it back in England. The next day we flew back to Buenos Aires, had a very good flight and arrived on time. Much to our delight our local guide was again Maria Irma. We had a short visit back to the hotel and then were taken to

San Telmo to the market which is only on Sundays. We were given plenty time to look round and buy coffee if we wished. We had a Chinese lady in our group who normally fell asleep while on the coach, but on this occasion she was in her element. She had found somewhere to buy quirky spectacle frames. She wore very outlandish ones, but they suited her. She hadn't realised what type of trip this was when she booked it. There were all sorts of stalls selling antiques and curiosities, and people dancing street tango, in tiny areas because on Sunday at the market it is so busy. The sound of the guitars playing the tango music, and the whole atmosphere was wonderful. After that we were taken to La Recoleta, the cemetery where Eva Peron is buried, and it was explained that families have special days when they go to their families graves and have picnics. There is always a flower on Eva Peron's grave, which is in a structure like a mausoleum. A lot of the graves are like that.

We had earlier been shown the Pink Palace in the city where the balcony is that Eva Peron spoke to the people from. This is the official residence of the President of Argentina.

We were being taken later for a tango show at El Viejo Almacen Tango followed by a dinner, which was truly wonderful as we had seats right in front of the stage, the music was wonderful and this is when the description of the small accordion was given as it had been developed for this music. A spellbinding performance, we were told a lot of the dancers had been trained in ballet. We then crossed a street and went into a lovely restaurant for a splendid dinner, which more music was played for us as we ate.

The last morning had arrived, we were given free time so some of us went to the H. Stern shop as we had been given a voucher for a charm. I ended up being tempted as having bought a bracelet and ring at Iguazu with different coloured stones, here were even nicer earrings.

Well what was a girl supposed to do? You got it, go shopping.

That afternoon there was a trip on the Tigre Delta which was on board a lovely wooden boat and took us up past all the islands which had formed by the silt, and had been built on, some of the houses were very elaborate, and an original house has been covered in clear material so it can be seen but not deteriorate, as it is of historic importance, as the man who built it has left an extensive library in it. Some of the birds on the Delta were lovely, saw Egrets wading. All the houses had jetties, and at one point we saw a little shop and fuel station for the boats on one of the islands. The boat we were on does a school run for the children, as well as the families having their own boats. Three neighbouring jetties had names for the Three Musketeers, Porthos, Artemis and Athos.

On the way to the Delta and also on the way back, we had the Presidents country house pointed out to us, as while in the city we had seen the Pink Palace. Back to the hotel, off to the Airport, and the end of a most wonderful journey, and a promise kept to my Mum to thank Luis Alberto Lazo.

Chapter 11

Australia 2008   Ayrshire to Australia

The next adventure came about, as when Mum was 90, I
had decided the occasion needed celebrating and just
after we had got back from the Saga Rose her cousin
had arrived from Australia, as I had let her know we were
having a big party. I had managed to keep this from
Mum until we were on the plane to Tenerife for that trip.
While Janet was here from Australia, she had said I must
come and visit sometime. So realising that she and her
husband were having a 50th wedding anniversary party, I
decided that my cousin Catriona and I should try and go.
Catriona had to get permission to be off her work for a
whole month, and once she got it, we got booked to go
from Glasgow to Singapore via London, and had a
stopover in Singapore which enabled us to have a visit to
the Night Safari, at the Zoo. British Airways had come
up trumps, as they had booked us into the Fairmont
Hotel, and organised a driver to meet us at the airport.
However when trying to get all the trips in Australia

organised I realised that I needed the services of a Travel Agent, as I could not book the interior trips. Fortunately a travel agent had opened in West Kilbride where I live, LAH Travel, so I went and spoke to Linda Hill and explained that I had been so smart booking flight direct with BA but now had this problem. Linda looked into it and said she could book the APT trips as they could only be done through an ABTA registered agent. She also amazingly got the BA flights linked to internal flights so we got the package for them. After that I decided any future holiday I am arranging will be done through her business, as it saves so much hassle.

On arrival at Singapore a driver was there to meet us as arranged and Edwin as he was called had asked what we would like to do in Singapore. We told him, and he waited while we got checked in and then took us to the Zoo, waited for us and took us back to the hotel.

He gave us a price for getting us tickets for Sentosa Island's attractions and getting there by cable car, so we told him to go ahead and come for us next morning after breakfast.

Edwin started by taking us to a temple to see a golden Buddha, and a Goddess of fertility, which highly amused Catriona and me as our families are grown up. We were then taken up to where the Cable Car was and Edwin provided us with packets of nuts, bottles of orange juice and water, and tissues, and gave us a mobile phone to call him if we needed help, also an umbrella in case of a downpour.

He told us he would phone in the afternoon when he had driven over to Sentosa Island to meet up with us, and gave us all the tickets we would need for the Butterfly Garden, which is also a Parrot Sanctuary, which we enjoyed going around and seeing the lovely butterflies.

We went to the IMAX cinema and had the full 4D experience in a film about pirates. As this was new and innovative we had not been at anything like that before. Cinema seat moving getting sprayed with water, it was great fun. We then went to the Images of Singapore Museum about life in Singapore from the start, through the Japanese occupation, and to present times. It was fascinating, and a great museum. At this point Edwin phoned to say he was at the Merlion. We walked down a hill to the Merlion, and met him. We left him holding hats and shopping bags, while we climbed up into the Merlion and went out on the top to see the view over the South China Sea.

There are islands out there with oil storage tanks on them, which we could see in the distance, as well as all the oil tanker ships.

He then walked with us through an area with the most wonderful mosaics, and then took us to the car and back into Singapore to the Hotel. It was a marvellous outing.

We then went from the hotel through to a shopping mall and first shop we saw Marks and Spencer's. We had a wander there and saw a wonderful waterfall which as we passed it showed the date and time, it was a fleeting glimpse but is a feature of this waterfall. Quite amazing, we stood for ages hoping it would happen again, but it didn't.

That night we flew on to Australia, arriving at 4.00am and going through customs were told we hadn't filled in our forms correctly, I told the guy they were difficult to see in the cabin lighting, and was sorry about that, he said you're not the first and you won't be the last, to which I replied no my cousin has done the same and she is behind me. Thanks for the welcome to Australia, my grandfather is buried in Melbourne, the retort to this was Oh welcome I came out here from Scotland, the usual "Oh, where did you live conversation then started". Once we had retrieved our luggage and were through in the arrival area, the sniffer dogs had a good sniff and the handler asked if we had any food, we said no we ate it all on the plane, before we were sprayed! He then asked if we were staying long and where were we going to visit, everyone was surprised at what we were planning to pack in.

We then got a taxi to take us to our hotel, which when we got there had none of the rooms ready for the influx, we sat about with a lot of other people, until eventually we were told we could go and get some breakfast, then about 11.00 our room was ready. We thought we might go and have a lie down, but after having a cup of tea, we revived and set off sight- seeing. We went on the Monorail which was still there then got off at Darling Harbour, we worked our way back eventually, and then thought a hop on hop off bus tour would be good, so went for that the next day. It was great as it got us to all the different areas with the history of the city being explained as we went along.

In the area called the Rocks, we found a pub and sat on a roof terrace enjoying the view of the Harbour Bridge.

Our tickets were valid for two days so next day got out to the Opera House and went in to see it.   There was a display with lovely tutus from the Nutcracker Suite. We were very impressed with the marble in the ladies toilets as the basins were a design marvel in themselves, a continuous wavy line tilted to the wall so excellent drainage, automatic taps and soap dispenser, and paper towel dispensers above this!

Then we went and had a walk through the Botanic gardens and saw the Governors House.

That night we met up with my daughter-in-law's brother at Darling Harbour and he suggested we go to the Telecom Tower for our meal, so we went and booked a time, and as we had plenty time to wait, then went to a bar which was in a former bank, and downstairs. I have since seen it on a TV advert, for Australian wine. It was very quirky.

The next day we were off to the airport to fly to Wagga Wagga known as Wagga, where our cousin and her husband were meeting us. As soon as we got into the town they took us for coffee and cakes, and we had a great chat, as we hadn't seen Alan for years as Janet had come on her own to see my mother.

We then went on to Griffith where they live, and they were telling us that it is not only at the Ports and Airports that the no food rule applies but on state borders, and in the case of their area, there are check points between towns, as it is a fruit growing area, and vineyard area too. Janet was hoping they wouldn't be stopped as she remembered she had an apple in the car.

The next day Janet took us into the town and showed us around, and then told us how to get to the motel their son Ian and his wife Carolyn ran, so we set off and said we would see her back at the house. We saw Ian and Carolyn, and then after Carolyn gave us directions to get back we set off but... we missed something and we walked and walked and walked, and couldn't recognise anything, so I suggested that we should at the first turn go right and do the same each time we found a junction and hopefully that would get us back. Eventually as it was starting to get dark, and we were outside a retirement village with a name, we phoned Janet and Alan and said where we were. We were miles away, as Alan said gone bush!

We had seen parts of the Griffith area visitors normally don't! No harm done Alan came and got us and I was teased about that for the rest of our visit.

The next day our cousin Jim from New Zealand arrived which was lovely as we hadn't seen him for many years, it was like when we were kids again, as that was the last time the three of us had been together, and later our other cousin Jean and her husband Neville arrived, so the party was growing, Catriona, Jim and I were all staying with Janet and Alan, and Jean and Neville were staying at the Motel. They came over every day, and one day Jean, Catriona and I went into town and found a shoe sale, so we indulged. It was funny buying Italian sandals in an Australian town, but they were lovely. We then went to a Park area where we saw an Emu, and a young kangaroo that are being cared for there as they had been injured and would not survive in the wild now. Later Janet took us and showed us the Hermit's Cave where a Hermit lived long ago, and had his separate areas for his sleeping and his kitchen. He lived there many years.

There is a wine made in the area called Hermit's Cave and very good it is too. Unfortunately it doesn't come to the UK.

We got taken to the local Agricultural Show which was a chance to get up close with some Merino Sheep; they have got very thick fleeces, which when you sink your hands into the fleece you are covered in lanolin. We also met some baby alpacas which were adorable. The trucks were enormous, and Alan had put his treasured motor bike in a vintage motor bike display

The colours in the trees were beautiful, as it was their autumn, which we were forgetting with it being May.

Finally the day of the party arrived and we got all dressed up and went over to Ian and Carolyn's home and met their other son Stephen and his family who had travelled down from Forster for the event. It was a brilliant evening, and the food was gorgeous and the wine and beer flowed It was lovely meeting friends of the family who remembered my parents visiting, so all in all a very happy occasion.

The day after we went out to see where Janet and Jean had grown up on their Dad's fruit farm. We heard that a lot of these properties are being sub divided and used for building, as the supermarkets are only taking perfect un blemished fruits for sale and any with even the slightest mark can only be used for juices. So it is not viable to continue fruit farming. We picked up a grapefruit which had fallen and Catriona and I had it next day for breakfast, it was delicious. We then went to see where Janet and Alan had their farm, which was not a fruit farm but grew crops, before they retired and I was amazed at the colour of the soil as it was red.

Next morning Jean and Neville loaded us and our luggage into their car and drove us to Queensland over dirt roads and through areas you can't take a hire car, so we saw the non -tourist areas.

Some of the old colonial architecture was reminiscent of pictures of the Deep South in USA. The wrought ironwork was very intricate.

Some of the place names we passed through were old Aboriginal like Goondawindi and Toowomba. They took us through the Jimna Rainforest and stopped at a couple of viewpoints which had stunning views for miles. We asked Neville why he always drove up the middle of the road, and he said to avoid kangaroos. At this point we hadn't seen any, and when he explained this he said to shout out if we saw any, just with that I said that looks like one up ahead and it was sitting bang slap in the middle of the road. Reasoning which was dubious. We were very fortunate to see as much as we did.

Later in the journey we stopped when we saw a wonderful reflection in the McIntyre River of all the trees on the bank. It was reminiscent of Scotland and the lochs on a still day.

We stopped at motels overnight, and at Inglewood we got a flashlight from the motel owner and he told us to go down to the dump as kangaroos were known to go raiding there at night. We didn't see any kangaroos but did see a white frog mouthed owl which was very large. One town we visited was Cowra, where we visited the Japanese Garden, which was a joint venture between the Australian and Japanese Governments, and is a beautiful place to visit. It is a wonderful tribute to forgiveness. Very calming!

We had quite a few interesting stops, and near the end of the journey we stopped in a town called Kilcoy because they have a shop which makes very good pies. True, we tested them and agreed they were excellent.

Our breakfasts were hard boiled eggs we had brought with us and crackers and cheese, as they had a fridge in the car, and all the motel rooms have fridges, obviously necessary for the Australian temperatures. We visited many towns en- route and saw so many things.

While we were with Jean and Neville, we went to Noosa Heads and had a walk in the town which is an attractive town, and has some lovely restaurants, we had lunch at a fish restaurant which was overlooking the river afterwards going for a ferry ride up the Noosa River to the Sheraton Hotel which is the point for disembarking the ferry.

We also took the chance to go to Australia Zoo at Brisbane, and there is a free bus from Noosa to the Zoo.

What an amazing place that is, and the animal welfare and research is world famous. We saw the Crocoseum, and wonderful animals with loads of space to roam including Tigers with cubs.

The Elephants were taken for a walk and the children given apples to give to them. They did belong to a circus but now live at the Zoo, although still owned by the circus family. They are extremely well cared for.

As you walk from one section to another, you open a gate and when it is closed you then walk out another gate so the animals can't get from one section to another, Airlock system I suppose. As we were walking where there were Koalas I was delighted to fine one dozing in a tree, so gave it a little stroke.

The variety of the animals and the display at the Crocoseum was terrific. We had walked round the crocodiles earlier and some of them were enormous.

When we got back Jean and Neville had heated up the Spa which we called a Jacuzzi, I had a quick swim but the pool was cold, so we jumped into the spa and Neville gave us glasses of champagne. We then moved into the

Cabana they had and we had a lovely dinner of party food, a brilliant evening.

We were moving on from there so Neville drove us into Brisbane to the Airport, and he was so busy showing us the city we nearly missed our flight. Of course rushing to get through a spot check was required on my bag, and I nearly dropped everything trying to repack it, and we just made it onto the plane. Once on board and settled for our flight to Cairns, the stewardess and steward were asking what we had done and where all we were going, and how long were we staying in Australia, then when they brought a snack of muffins, I felt something sharp in my mouth and discovered a bit of metal, so called them to show them. They offered me another one which I declined, but said they would do something about it on their way home as they passed the suppliers place on their way home.

Five minutes later she came back again with a bottle of Champagne by way of an apology, which I did accept. We enjoyed it later in our room.

The hotel room we got was an upgrade, and had a balcony, a kitchen area, as well as a sitting area. It was a mini suite.

It transpired there were a couple of coachloads of Japanese, so they wanted to them to have their rooms together, so that was our good fortune. There was also a super laundry on the premises, so we were able to get our clothes washed and I discovered that Catriona was good at ironing, I offered but was told she would do it, talk about travelling with the perfect companion.

We were amazed at the number of school trips that were passing our hotel as we sat out on our balcony in the evening, and they seemed to be Oriental children chattering away in in their language, not sure whether Chinese or Japanese.

While in Cairns, we did a trip on the cable car up to Kuranda, flying over the canopy of the trees. We were taken to an outdoor theatre where we saw an aboriginal display then were taken to a field for a lesson in boomerang throwing, some of our party were better than others, I was rubbish, then we had a look at part of the rain forest, and were able to see the animals. We were offered the chance to hold a real Koala, mine was called Humphrey he was a lovely big boy.

We went to get something to eat, afterwards got a trip on an Army Duck on the lake, the trees and vines were explained to us. Fan palms are slow growing and we were shown a fairly small one to our eyes when we were told it was 500 years old!

The Kuranda Railway to Cairns is an amazing railway snaking its way down through the rainforest and the views are spectacular. The cable car on the way up had been constructed so carefully none of the trees were removed or damaged. It is a UNESCO world heritage site.

After arriving back in Cairns and wandering our way back to our hotel, which was easy as Cairns is built as a grid; we got changed and went out to eat. We found a restaurant right down at the esplanade called Villa Romano, and our waiter Stephano was from Barcelona, so I got to practice my Spanish! We had a lovely meal there.

Next morning up again bright and early, to be picked up for a trip to the Barrier Reef, drove to Port Douglas along the beautiful coast road. Very pretty harbour and we went out on Quicksilver 5 an aluminium catamaran, similar to the one at the Glaciers in Argentina.

This journey took an hour and a half to the pontoon at Atherton Reef, 40 km offshore, where there were facilities for diving, snorkelling and going in a glass bottomed boat which was our choice. We saw wonderful coral, some like cauliflowers, cabbage and saw sea cucumbers. Hundreds of little silver fishes, also very colourful yellow butterfly fish, kiss me quick fish and boulder coral. We also saw a turtle and a small shark.

Lunch was on the boat but we took plates across to the pontoon to eat. The food was salads with various cold meats, chicken legs, pasta, all very tasty a lovely relaxing day.

The water was surprisingly cold; some of the divers were shivering when they came on board. Once back in Cairns we had a quick dash to a shop to get the memory card photos put on to a CD, so we could start again!

We then got our washing done and chilled out on our balcony with nibbles and wine, our nibbles included Weetabix with avocado dip spread on them! Different, but that was what we had to hand.

22nd May now and pick up was at 7.15am, drove up the coastal road with Coral Sea looking beautiful to Daintree where we stopped for morning tea at the Habitat which included fruit and cakes. We got to see more of Australia's animals, and opted to go and see Kangaroos and wallabies which are very tame as expect the visitors to feed them. Lots of different species of wallabies, tiny nail tailed ones; a little later saw a joey being cleaned by his mother. Very endearing! There were also very small very dark brown ones, and saw one being attacked by an Ibis but it then picked on another wallaby. Lots of other animals, but as we had already seen most of them, just took our time with the wallabies and looking for the tree kangaroos, which we eventually spotted.

We then went out into the forest and had a walk with a guide telling us about the trees and vines which had invaded the centre of some of the trees till they are killed; you could see the hole through the tree. Further along we were shown a vine wrapped tree, which will be choking to death.

They also warned us about the "wait a while" vine which is like Velcro and catches on clothes. The Rattan vine is hollow and can be filled with water, while looking at all this we saw blue Ulysses butterflies which are gorgeous. We also saw a pelican which was quite close.

168

Lunch was at the Daintree Lodge where we had salads, meats, chicken, fruit, and those who wanted to could swim in the pool. We went for a wander down onto the beach, and just had a paddle along the edge in the lovely warm water, unlike the colder temperature out on the reef, while looking at the famous Cape Tribulation, as named by Captain Cook when he was caught there in a storm.

We were told that ninety percent of coffee is grown on tablelands and Daintree tea is grown in an area of forest. The Mountain at Cape Tribulation is called Mount Sorrow, not surprising given the history of this Cape. The trees grow right down to the water's edge onto the sand, and Daintree is the oldest rainforest in the world.

Once lunch and wandering came to a halt we were then taken on a river trip where we saw one male, two females and a baby crocodile basking. We also could see small snakes up on branches of the trees at the water edge just sunning. We also saw Egrets and a Spoonbill. The local language is Kukai, and the different tribes have different languages. After the river trip we were given coffee and biscuits, and while enjoying that saw a beautiful golden orchid growing up a tree.

We retraced our steps a bit and then were taken to another beautiful bay and got another beach walk, and a walk to a viewpoint en-route we saw a lace monitor in the undergrowth also a huge spider which I am glad to say was in its web! Our driver/guide told us that the breadfruit originated in Tahiti and came in the time of Captain Cook.

En-route back to Cairns we were taken to a farm, where those that wished could buy the ice-cream made there, they had five minutes to get it. This was an unscheduled treat courtesy of the driver. We stopped briefly later at a viewpoint, where on the Reef trip we had seen hang-gliders.

We took our things back to the hotel and then went and found a lovely little Greek taverna, which as it wasn't open, asked if there were any other restaurants like that nearby and were directed to the Adelfia which is run by the Andre brothers. We had a brilliant meal of lamb cutlets, washed down with Greek wine and finishing with a small glass of retsina. After the meal the waiter explained that the Andre brothers had a famous brother in the UK Peter Andre.

Next job after the lovely meal was to go and get packed up for the next instalment of our adventure to Alice Springs. A car came to collect us next morning at 9.50am took us to the airport where we had no problems checking in and going through to departures, went for a coffee and for a third time met a Vietnamese family we had met on previous day trips, who were from Edmonton in Canada.

We had met them over these different trips. They were going to Sydney, so we sat with them for a little while and bade them farewell as our flight was called. We were the first to board and had front seats. The stewardesses asked us where we had been and were amazed at the amount we had seen and what we had seen, some of that being courtesy of Jean and Neville

taking us to places off the tourist trails and onto dirt

roads.

Chapter 12

The Red Centre and back to Scotland

Approaching Alice Springs and looking out the plane window all we could see was an arid desert landscape but very flat with scrubby bushes.

At Alice there was a young girl to meet us and take us to Heavitree Gap Motel, which we had opted for rather than a hotel in town, as the McDonnell ranges are on the edge of the town where the Motel is and the rock wallabies come down at night and up close. You buy special pellets from reception. I got a bit annoyed one night at a family who were letting the children feed them bread, so I explained that is people food and that the pellets are not expensive. They were very good and got the right stuff.

Catriona burst out laughing when she saw our room, as it was like a room on a school trip, one double bed, and bunks, but when we opened the door we only saw the bunk beds. However we had a little hob, a kettle a fridge, so we could go to the onsite supermarket and get ourselves stuff for snacks and breakfast, and there was a decent restaurant for dinner which was reasonably priced. The only thing we had to watch was that the Aborigines sleep in the open in the area, and the supermarket was patrolled to stop them buying too much alcohol. Sadly a lot of them have white man's troubles with the drink. They also leave rubbish, they call it white man's rubbish, like polybags, originally they left leaves etc. in their culture all natural materials were used before white man introduced plastic, so now they are only doing what they always did, except the material is no longer a degradable one. It will take time for them to be educated as many still are not adapted to our western culture. Who is right or wrong?

At about 5.00 in the evening the wallabies start to come down off the red rocks, and come quite close, putting their little "paws" up asking for food, we dropped it to the ground as not sure if they would bite. One had a little joey peeping out of her pouch and she spent a lot of time with us. She nibbled my toes but it didn't hurt. They are only about 12 inches high, and most endearing marsupials. They crop grass a lot.   We also saw a grey kangaroo one night which was a lot bigger and came quite close.

In the hotel bistro they had a resident entertainer, who sang and did a show, but also played Rod Steward CD's. He came over and spoke to us and said his family had come from Southampton to Adelaide in the 1950's; he still had traces of South of England in his accent. We said we would go to his show the next night. Both Catriona and I are finding writing our journals great but fear we are now having gaps as so much to remember.

Next morning not having got up too early, given we have been on a whistle-stop journey, we went over to "Old Alice" which is the breakfast room, where we had a lovely breakfast to set us up for the day. We also spoke to the guy who didn't know that next day we needed early breakfast at 6.15 am before our pickup for onward journey, at 6.50am. However, although laid back he was very happy to make that arrangement.

We sat out but even at 10.00am still chilly as the sun now only starting to come over the Range. Some wallabies came to see us but we weren't going to feed them till tonight. They are cheeky little marsupials.
We thought we heard a Kookaburra calling but it didn't seem as raucous as ones we heard previously, so wonder if it was a different bird.

Our driver today is Laurie who picked us and six others up and first off took us to Anzac Hill a memorial to the Australian soldiers, the view from there was incredible as we could see all around Alice and the total area it covers, larger that we had imagined.

Next stop was the Royal Flying Doctor centre, so interesting, and brought home the isolation of the families living out in the bush. We spent quite some time there and were fascinated by the display of old medical equipment, especially the original plane compared to the modern one!

We were also shown a map showing the area covered by the Royal Flying Doctors which is enormous. From Alice to Yulara the Uluru town formerly called Ayers Rock up to Tennant Creek 600 km.

We were then taken to a Gallery of Aboriginal work, the Mbantua Gallery, we spent a little time there and admired the paintings, and indigenous craft work. Next stop was to the School of the Air, which was tremendous, and showed how then using radio the children in the outback were educated, and now it is with the use of the Internet, and this means they can see their teachers.

They have a get together at least once a year when the children are brought into town, and meet each other. Indeed it is a marvellous way of making sure the children learn, and do not feel isolated. They have a map on the wall with photographs of all the children and every so often they are brought into town to meet up and some older ones board at school in term time. The school sends out packs to the children every two weeks and a tutor or parent works with them. They use whiteboards, and computers and the children send in their homework by email, but every so often have to submit tests handwritten so their written work is being checked. We heard a recording of what it used to be like over the radio with all the attendant crackles and hums of the transmission.

We then returned to the small coach transporting us and were taken out to the Old Telegraph Station, where we were told the first telegraph poles were wood and didn't last as the termites ate them, so they had to be replaced by metal poles.

We met Alex Ross, whose mother was white and who gave him up, he was adopted by a white family in Sydney and lived there, married a white woman, and only after his wife died did he and his three sons come back to live in Alice. He has stayed, his sons returned to Sydney.

He said that on one occasion people visiting the station insisted he must be one of the stolen children, but he said no his mother was not forced to give him up; she did it voluntarily to give him a better chance. He then told us the story of the stolen children is about the half- caste children who were brought by their mother's to the Methodist Mission who cared for them, and the mothers were allowed to visit every day, then they wanted to stay overnight with their children, which was impossible as there was no room. One night the children were all gathered up and taken in the dark to Cookstown, so when their mothers came the next day everyone had gone. The story is now well known.

We went back to Heavitree Gap and discovered that it was indeed named by an early surveyor working on the Telegraph Station who had asked if he could name it when he found it and was given permission to do so, which is why it is called after the Primary school he went to in Devon. Heavitree is an area in Exeter.

That night as promised we went to the Bistro for our meal and had Barramundi and chips, Aussie fish and chips! The guy we had spoken to sang and did a comedy turn which was a bit blue but we were in Australia, and it was very funny.   We left before the Karaoke.

We got our early breakfast and were ready for the coach taking us to the Kings Canyon Ranch; we stopped and had a coffee Mount Ebenezer, where some of our fellow passengers had a Camel ride. We refrained; we had a wander round the animals and watched a couple of farm hands having a race on camels. There was also a dingo chained up, he was the guard dog! We went back on the coach till we reached a junction in the middle of nowhere, this was our drop off point, and there was a Land Rover waiting. This was Tony who had come from Kings Canyon Ranch to pick us up. His Grandfather had emigrated from Greenock on the West Coast of Scotland, near where we live.

We drove for a while and then stopped at Kings Creek Station, where we had coffee and a camel burger, I have never seen a burger that size before or since, it included a fried egg, pineapple and salad!

This is owned by the Conways, he had before this taken us to where Ian Conway had started his tourist business, and then when the landowner refused to renew his lease, Ian bulldozed it two hours before his lease ran out, as the landowner had thought he would just take over the business Ian had spent years building up. He then got land further over, and has now extended as being part Aborigine he is entitled to extra allocations of land. He has cattle but is now one of three Australians who have a licence to export camels to Arab countries. The first camels came to the country from the Canary Islands and the cameleers were from Afghanistan, India and Pakistan, to carry food and materials for building the original Ghan Railway, hence its name.

Tony also took us to see a grave in the middle of nowhere of Mrs Abon, who when she died it took a week to get a policeman from Alice to pronounce her dead, and she was buried beside her homestead which is now gone.

After our burgers Tony spoke to a driver of an APT coach which had broken down, we heard later they got back to Cairns at 11.30pm. We went on to the Outback Lodge where we were staying, in tents, we were given a cold drink, then taken to our "tent" complete with hot and cold running water, proper bathroom with shower, beds, and a wooden deck with table and chairs. Glamping is the word. We freshened up and then were taken to the Canyon and did the Gorge Walk for an hour and saw amazing birds and plants, too numerous to remember and did not have pen and paper with me. We had hats with nets over them to stop the bugs.

Before dinner everyone met on the deck for drinks and nibbles, and dinner was barbeque beside a fire pit, in front of the Lodge, some of the lights were flame some rechargeable Coleman lamps, the menu was shrimps, kangaroo, beef, barramundi with baked potatoes, salad, mixed roasted vegetables, mushrooms, and washed down with wine, Australian of course, an excellent meal.

After the meal we were taken to the other side of the house and given star gazing lessons, as the desert sky was perfect for that. We saw Saturn and its moons through the telescope, and the Southern Cross was so visible, a magical evening. Then it was a complimentary port and off to bed. It was a cold night but the beds were cosy and there were lovely fluffy blankets on top. Breakfast was served indoors at 6.45am at the kitchen. Tony took us out in the Land Rover over the station, and showed us Petroglyphs which are 8.000 years old. He showed us that an arrow pointing upwards was the sign for Emu, two downward strokes with ticks outwards at the base was Kangaroo, a circle meant Place, and a small foot which meant a child was there. He also showed us a stone with a hollow and a stone which would have been used to grind berries or similar on the stone with the hollow worn by grinding. He then took us and showed us fences with tinnies tied on, beer, gin and tonic all sorts, the cans are tied onto the barbed wire fences to stop the camels from damaging the fences a lot of the drinks at the Ranch are in cans. We were helping with the fence supplies while there!

There was also a double fenced area with a gap between, which is a quarantine area. The exported camels are wild camels which are caught and are healthier than the native ones in Dubai, Saudi Arabia etc. and are exported there to improve the bloodlines and health of the Arab camels.

That brought our visit to the Lodge and Station to an end and we returned to the Lodge to collect our bags and Tony took us back to the corner of the highway to meet up with that day's APT tour coach, which took us on to Yulara, the resort for Uluru, formerly known as Ayers Rock. We quickly checked in, put our stuff in our room, and then back on the coach for a trip to the Olgas, amazing rocks some of which have petroglyphs in them if you look closely. We had a scramble about and looked at the amazing formations of these truly ancient rocks, and went up a gorge between some of them, some of them are rocks on their sides as millions of years ago they fell over.

After that we were advised to move quickly to the facilities as there were three coachloads of Japanese tourists approaching we were also warned that these are Long Drop Toilets, do not let anything of value go down, as never to be seen again!

That night we went out to Uluru to watch the sunset and have drinks while enjoying the spectacle, before going on to have a Barbeque in the desert. Uluru goes a lovely purple shade just before dark. Dark is like the lights being switched off, total blackness.

We were the only non -Japanese at the barbeque as the rest of the party were however much sign language and smiling did the trick.

This time the menu was chicken, kangaroo, lamb, sausage, and beef with salads, and pasta and wine.

Well why not we were on holiday. We were back at the hotel at 8.30 and off to bed and in the morning we had to be up at 5.00am for pick up at 5.30am to go to see the sunrise at Uluru. Once the colour starts it is a brown/orange and then goes to a most brilliant rose then gold. What a stunning sight.

We took breakfast with us using the Lammington cakes a cake with coconut which seems to be an Aussie delicacy. They were very good and we had saved from the previous evening and coffee was provided by the coach. It seemed ages in the dark, then slowly a slight rose tint started then spread then the most glorious rose colour engulfed the rock and then turned it gold before going to its glorious red. Something which cannot be adequately described, but should be experienced.

At dusk the night before it had looked purple, it is indeed a magical place. From there we were taken nearer, and told certain areas are sacred so photography is forbidden, but in other areas perfectly permissible. We did the Mala walk saw a waterhole and cave paintings thousands of years old. As you go along there are signs where the story is related to you as you pass by recordings, really well set up.

We saw a sacred area where the rock looks like a wallaby pouch where pregnant women go to rub their abdomens against the rock for a safe pregnancy. Further along we could see how the cave was formed as a sleeping area screened by rock, and a food preparation area to the front. There were also many types of Eucalyptus trees, and it was explained to us that some lose limbs stop them from dying when it is a long drought. The whole area doesn't get much rain ever. The Aborigines were very good at land management and burned areas to keep fire to a minimum. The powers that be are now realising that fire breaks burned deliberately are one way of stopping bush fire spreading.

We were then taken to a Cultural Centre where a great many things were explained to us. The different tribes operate in different ways, and the famous digeridoo is not used in Central Australia, as they clack boomerangs together to make music. They have a boomerang shaped like a number 7 which they use to break animals legs so they don't kill them to keep them fresh till the animal can be got to their camp. The women dig for witchety grubs in the roots of the witchety bush. There is also a bush called "almost finished" which has hard spiky leaves and the aborigines push into a wart then break it off and leave the end in and it cures them. They also boil it up and make a liniment from it.

We returned to our hotel aptly named the Outback Pioneer and had free time till 4.50pm.

I first saw a photo of this hotel when my parents stayed there in 1978, it has been modernised, but it was lovely to see where my parents had visited. We were at 4.50 picked up by AAT Kings coaches and taken out into the desert. In a square set out we were greeted by waiters with glasses of champagne, and canapes of crocodile, kangaroo, and salmon. All very interesting and tasty, the croc was quite a fishy taste not surprisingly. We watched the sun set on Uluru and again a magical experience, not just a sight to behold, but a true experience. While this was happening there was a man playing a digeridoo and it was truly lovely to hear the haunting tones while the sun was going down. What a sound, from an amazing instrument

We were then led along a lit path to a place where tables had been set and there was a kitchen.

We sat with a couple from Birmingham, Diana and Philip on an extended holiday, all the way from the UK to the Australian desert and met other Brits! Shows what travellers we are from our island. The tables were set for eight, the others were Clare and Kevin who were caravanning around Oz, and were staying on the campsite, and Kerry and Nancy who like us are on holiday. The setting was magical, candles on the tables, and patio heaters so we didn't get cold as at night in the desert it can be very cold. The digeridoo player was a white man called Dwayne and he was a friend of the local tribe and had permission to play. He explained about the Digeridoo and how it is the oldest instrument in the world, he also explained how the termites eat the centre of the tree and that now some instruments are made by boring them with tools; he stressed not the real thing, and does not give the same sound.

The meal was carrot and coriander soup, followed by chicken, barramundi, beef, emu, kangaroo, and salads, potatoes and pasta, from a buffet style servery. There were puddings but by that time we were full up. While we were up getting our main course our linen napkins were refolded and our wine glasses refilled, indeed as if by magic!

After the meal had finished, they put out all the lights and the fire-pit, and gave us a talk about the stars. It was truly incredible to see all the stars so clearly, that was three consecutive nights we had been able to see all the stars including the Southern Cross which is kite shaped in the southern hemisphere, with the various constellations being pointed out.

After that we were asked to stop all conversation and invited to listen to the Sound of Silence! It was true silence, in total darkness, and another wonderful experience, not the crack of a twig, or a leaf falling there was total silence. Magical!

On re-boarding our coach we were given a ticket to go to the hotel called the "Sails in the Desert" for a free drink. We didn't demur, some of our party were by this time a bit wobbly to say the least, but what the heck, when are any of us going to be back to do this again, a once in a lifetime thrill this trip was proving to be one of these! We had our drink and enjoyed being able to see what it is like at $2.000aus per night, lovely but we will not be booking any time as out of our budget!

Our trip to Australia was rapidly coming to a close, and on the 28th we cleared our room, and put our cases into the porter's room after having a cheese roll, a mandarin orange and juice for breakfast. We went and sat at the pool and read to put in the time till we would be picked up for the airport. The souvenir T shirts had been bought for the family. We were picked up at midday and check in took a little while due to a group of Japanese who were also being checked in, probably our companions from the BBQ in the desert. We had good seats on the plane and were with Diana and Philip we had met at the Sound of Silence dinner in the desert. We had to sit on the tarmac at Sydney till a storm passed as all the ground staff had been called in due to the danger of lightening. We got our bags and then found the shuttle bus for the Radisson, as I had decided we were having a real treat to finish our Australian Odyssey. Bus was a bit chaotic, but when we got to the hotel, we were greeted with a quick check in, freshened up and went for a dinner in their Bistro restaurant. Trina ordered veal and I chose duck both absolutely perfect. We had been given complimentary potato soup to start with. The hotel is beautiful, and when arranging the trip, I had decided to do inexpensive at the start and we would finish with a bang, as the chances of repeating it were nil.

We had a great sleep and just after waking Jean and Neville phoned and said goodbye and how great it was that we had visited. We had breakfast of fruit and cold meats, cheese, bread and croissants. We checked out at 10.15 and got the shuttle bus to airport, but before we left the Commissaire said if we ever wanted opals to let him know and he would get them for us. In that hotel if you said you wanted anything it would be got for you.

When we got to the airport we heard that Quantas was on strike, good job we were flying with good old BA.

We had a good flight and were met by another limousine at Singapore Airport, again arranged by British Airways, taken to the Fairmont again and arrived at 10.30pm. Once in room we did our maps that Jean had provided us with for all the parts of Australia we had covered, and then showered and went to bed.

We were up at 8.00am, and sorted out our cases and went for breakfast, all sorts of exotic fruits like dragon fruits, and more familiar apples and oranges, cold meats, cheeses. We got an extension on our room till 4.00pm as travelling late. After breakfast we got a taxi to take us to Orchard Road, where at the shopping mall we marvelled at all the designer handbags, which were literally wall to wall, how to choose. We opted not to as the choice was massive! The same applied to the shoes, and as for the jewellery, I think you needed an appointment, as it was absolutely stunning. Blindingly beautiful gems.

I did however buy a new case as mine had developed a problem. I seem to buy cases in foreign locations, as my red spinner was from Buenos Aires. However quite a good souvenir, and the price was right! We then went for lunch in the hotel, then were going on a pilgrimage to Raffles for a Singapore Sling, a must do situation. After again trying the local fare this time fruit and fish for lunch, we noticed an extremely black cloud overhead and lo and behold as we stepped out the hotel door, from the air conditioning, the thunder rumbled, the lightening cracked and the heavens opened, so we retreated into the lovely foyer of the Fairmont, and watched the rain cascade, people running with umbrellas up and waited till it abated which took about three quarters of an hour. When we made it across to Raffles, we discovered they had been hosting an outdoor wedding which had been quickly relocated inside, and it looked beautiful, we had a little wander marvelling at the old hotel and the lovely architecture and furnishing, then went to the famous Long Bar for our Slings, and to eat peanuts and drop litter in the only legal place in Singapore to do so. The slings were wonderful, expensive but worth it. We were regaled with the story that the peanut shells are dropped so when tigers would come they would hear them as the shells would crunch! True or not it's a good story. What a lovely place, and so clean not just Raffles, but Singapore. We could learn lessons from there.

We got photos with our Singapore Slings and did the same for a couple beside us. After we had finished them we went for a hot sticky walk round the malls at Raffles and had a look at the inside courtyards. We went back across the street again to the Fairmont and went to the shopping Mall accessible from the hotel, and had a wander as we had some time till being collected for the airport. After trying to get a cup of tea without success, we ended up in the spa and discovered we could have a shower and after that were taken for a lie down for half an hour and given ginger and honey tea which was delicious. That refreshed us as having had to give up our room, we had been very sticky. I went to do video of the beautiful flower arrangements in the foyer, when the driver came early as had been told the traffic was heavy and didn't want us to be late. I love this place. We were at the airport in plenty time and checked in immediately. We sat around and read after going through security. We had a good flight to London and got in at 6.10am on the 31st May a month after leaving Glasgow, we had a good look round the quite new Terminal 5 and had coffee and crisps, not quite the diet, we had been enjoying. We got to the boarding gate and were boarded quickly, then after take- off got a second breakfast which we were ready for.   Trina's sister and niece and my husband

were there to collect us, after we had eventually got our

luggage which had come off a different carousel.

Welcome back to Scotland.   That was a fabulous trip.

Chapter 13

Cruising again!

Think it is time to get back to cruising, that has been neglected for quite some time due to family commitments, moving house, grandchildren starting to arrive, and family weddings, as my family had decided to settle down, unlike their mother. The Maiden Baltic Cruise of Queen Elizabeth was selected for 2011, so back to LAH Travel and this time Sue got us all sorted out. We decided to go two days before and stay at the Ibis at Southampton, which was perfectly suitable for our purpose. We went by train and had opted to go first class. We set off from our local station, and my husband accompanied us to Glasgow and saw us over to the London train, which would take us as far as Wolverhampton where we were to change trains. Part of the deal with the train was that you got a meal included. The clause we hadn't seen was that did not happen on bank holidays, and yes it was a bank holiday. However the lady in charge of the trolley got us unlimited sandwiches, coffee and crisps.

When we got to Wolverhampton we also had booked assistance so our cases were lifted off for us and the good thing was as our train drew away, we just had to stay put as the platform was where the train to go cross country to Southampton would come in. Our luggage was lifted on for us and again we were to get assistance at Southampton to get them off, which was as well as my companion did not travel light. We got a taxi from the station to the Ibis and were soon in a very comfortable room. We spent the evening having something to eat, and then watched television. The next day we had arranged to get the train to Cosham and meet with a relation of mine, and go to her house for lunch. We had a lovely time with her and caught up with news, then time for us back to get the train back to Southampton. We spent the second night doing the same having a meal and a drink and watching television. The next day we got a taxi to take us to the port and did not have long to wait till we were boarded and in our stateroom awaiting our luggage. After we had attended the safety briefing and taken our lifejackets back to our room, we set off to explore this new ship, and get our bearings. Captain was Christopher Wells whose announcements were always delivered with humorous intonation. First port Kristiansand was cancelled, as the day we were due in Copenhagen there were a lot of cruises due in and we would go a day earlier, so first port was Oslo, and was so interesting, we went to the Thor Heyerdahl museum and saw Kontiki, Ra and other things associated with him. Then we went to the Viking ship museum and saw amazingly preserved Viking ships which had been burial ships, and some of the treasures recovered. It seemingly is because of the blue clay which they had been buried in that so much has survived and been excavated successfully.

A sleigh and other belongings were buried in the funeral ship.

The next port of Copenhagen was a repeat visit for my companion so I agreed we would not do a trip and we just walked about which was very pleasant and we walked into the centre of the town and saw the typical old yellow houses and a lovely statue with lions at the foot of it.

We then continued till we came to a street with a selection of lovely little cafés, so had a sit down and coffee before wandering back to the ship a different way and going past the little mermaid, which really is little, we had a look at shop artisan type shops on the quayside which had some lovely things in them.

On our return to the ship it was very poignant for me as Marco Polo the ship my mother had been on in Antarctica when she got pneumonia was moored next to us, and then we watched her sail away. We had re-boarded and at this point the announcement went out for particular passengers to identify themselves to the purser's office. This happens frequently when about to leave port as invariably someone is late back and perhaps the scanning in has not gone into the system. We are scanned off and scanned back for security purposes, and also for a headcount.

As Kristiansand had been cancelled we got a new port added in and this was Travemunde, in Lubeck Germany, we didn't see the welcome in the morning but heard about it and the sail away at night was amazing, as Queen Elizabeth was the largest ship they had ever had in to their port. During the day we got a trip to Hamburg and a coach trip round the city. There was a visit to a café where very strong coffee was served along with cake, I took the apple tart, a huge slice was put in front of me and I struggled to finish it, but it was delicious. They have statues of the Beatles in the centre of the city as they were so popular there. We were taken down the Reeperstrand which is now a respectable area but previously was the red light district, so we were told.

After returning to the ship at Travemunde, we got champagne to sip on deck while sailing away, and decided not to go for dinner as this was so exciting, there were thousands of people lining the sides of the river and small yachts and motor boats following us out. There were people standing on balconies with Union Jack flags draped over as well as a local band playing on the shore, they even played our national anthem.

When we got the mouth of the river and the beaches there were people standing on the sand and in the water, cheering and waving. We were cheering and waving back. An amazing experience, eventually we were in the open sea on our way to Stockholm. The trip in Stockholm to the ice bar was great and really interesting to see the engravings in the ice, also the vodka drunk from an ice glass was fun.

The tour round the city was lovely as sitting on the coach we could see plenty. I was on my own for that one too. However as our dinner table was in the stern and beside large windows, we were able to sit and have dinner as we made our way down the archipelago through the thousands of little islands with houses on them as some of them are holiday homes. What a truly memorable sight, all our table companions loved it. We had been sat with two couples, who were celebrating anniversaries, and were excellent company.

The trip in Helsinki left a lot to be desired as it was supposed to be a sleigh ride and other snowy things but turned out to be a trip to a warehouse with snow in it but decoration was skimpy and the whole thing most disappointing, we did get a partial refund. However while going through the city we did see a bit of it from the coach and some people got off at a shopping centre and were to make their own way back to the ship.

St Petersburg what an amazing city, the trip to Catherine Palace was spectacular, I thought if I never saw Gold leaf again I wouldn't worry, well the next day it was the trip to Peterhof. I ended up going myself again as the companion was not up to it, I very nearly missed the coach and the tour girl in the Queens Room radioed the coach to wait while I ran through the terminal to passport control grinned at the Russians as we had been told to do, and actually had them giggling at me in my rush. I skidded onto the coach and realised that I had run, first time since having my foot surgery. Hurrah my feet work. There was a spare seat beside a man who explained his wife had hurt her knee and couldn't come so we stuck together during the tour, and then on the Hydrofoil trip across the Bay of Finland back to St. Petersburg. The gardens at St. Petersburg are based on Versailles and absolutely beautiful, you cannot see everything in one visit, wonderful fountains some even quite amusing with ducks going around. The cascade is based on the one at Versailles and some say is more beautiful. The whole palace is amazing. We were told not to touch the gold leaf as we went up the stairs, but as usual one person just had to. Well one of the people from Peterhof was looking down from the landing, saw this and rapped on the bannister, saying "Niet". When we got into the room at the top of the stairs, our guide said to the person "Well that's you being sent to Siberia". Obviously they don't want it touched or it will wear away. The place is stunning and just too much to take in in a couple of hours.

Peterhof Palace is in a huge estate with a lovely terrace above the beautiful cascade which leads down to the Bay; we walked down past the cascade and boarded a hydrofoil there for a return trip to St. Petersburg, where our coaches were awaiting.

That night we were again in the city to the Hermitage where we were given a short tour through a few of the rooms, mainly looking at some rather dark religious type paintings, then shown into a most spectacular room with huge urn shaped vases covered in Malachite a very expensive mineral, which is why the vases are only covered in it, but a spectacular colour of green. We were having a concert by the St. Petersburg symphony orchestra. The programme was wonderful! There was a painting of St Mark's square by Canaletto on the wall beside me and I know there is one in the Royal

Collection in London! One of the pieces of music was from Eugene Onegin which was a favourite of my mother's and our evening finished with a glass of champagne.

Our next port was Tallinn, we were not on an organised tour, but just got off the shuttle bus and wandered up through a market, where there were stalls selling knitwear, clocks and ornaments, and where later I bought two sweaters for Christmas presents. This was May but was a good chance to get something different. We then went into the town through the old wall round the town and walked up through another market which seemed to be mainly flowers. Part of the town is very high and we decided not to try and walk too far. We found a restaurant with seats outside and were able to get a beer as it was warm, unwittingly we had picked the one where the ship shore trip were going to have their lunch, so the ships photographers took our photos too. I had noticed a lovely shop across the road, so once we had finished our drinks we went over and had a look in the shop, I had already bought a piece of amber for my step grand- daughter, and suddenly thought perfect for my three sons and daughters in law to get amber for their Christmas presents too, so cufflinks and pendants were purchased. I then bought a lovely poncho for the younger grand- daughter, as thought it would be cosy for her going to nursery. I would love to go back to Tallinn and be able to see more of the town, as only got to the square, especially as I took no photographs that day.

After disembarking the pilot that night our course was set south westerly back through the Baltic Sea passing to the south of Gotland and Oland at approximately 7am and 10.00am respectively. Captain Wells announced that we would be travelling through Fermanbelt at about 9.00pm before entering the Great Belts which are narrow passages between the many islands in the Baltic where there are often depths of less than 20 metres. He then said that he expected that the ship would pass under the Great Belt Bridge shortly before midnight. We didn't see it as we were too busy being entertained in the Queen's Room. We had another sea day the next day and then on the 13th June we were docking at Zeebrugge from where we were being taken to Ypres which was completely rebuilt after WWI. To see it now you would not know if compared to pictures of the original. It was rebuilt using the original mediaeval plans.

We had first been taken to a First World War battlefield and two War Cemeteries. These were very moving places to visit and the Tyn Cott Cemetery is huge which lets you see the horror of the loss of lives at the Somme and it is only one of the cemeteries. The second Cemetery was Essex Farm Cemetery and one grave in particular was heart rending.

Rifleman Strudwick had tried to sign up in his own village and had answered truthfully that he was 14; they said he was too young, so he walked to the next village and lied about his age so he could sign up. His birthday was not till later in January so when he was killed on the 14th January he was actually still only 14 years old, he may have been the youngest casualty of the Somme. We were told this by a young man who was with us as a guide. There were a lot of very young men buried in these places.

We also visited the Menin Gate where those who were listed as missing have their names engraved. There are thousands of names from all over the Commonwealth. There is also an area behind it where they have a model of the whole Menin Gate with braille plaques describing it so blind people can get an idea of its structure. I noticed one inscription the same as my surname which was under a Canadian Regiment, and then when you really look at all the different regiments named the enormity of the whole situation starts to hit home.

We then had sea days to get back to Southampton, and had lovely formal nights, and great entertainment. We had such a good time we decided to think about doing another cruise in a couple of years.

After much discussion, it was determined that I had to do a leg of a World Cruise so we booked to go on Queen Victoria from Dubai to Southampton in April 2013. As time progressed and shore trips were booked we got quite excited about it all. However as time got nearer half the shore trips had been cancelled due to the escalating situation in that part of the world, but Petra was still ok. I had one shore trip left. Due to an emergency with someone we knew my husband was standing in the freezing cold while another friend and I were trying to get the emergency services. These other friends had been about to depart to another part of the country to bid farewell to family emigrating, it was all rather fraught. My husband had been not well with a very bad head cold, but was on the antibiotics, however, fast forward to three days before we are setting off for Southampton, the poor man could hardly breathe, so this time it was him heading for the hospital. I am glad to say he recovered, but the trip was cancelled, my friend did not appreciate the severity at this point, as she had remarked could we see how things were in a couple of days. The insurance covered our losses and we then thought well we need to book something else.

Chapter 14

QM2 10th Anniversary crossing

A return to Cunard was booked for the 10th anniversary crossing of Queen Mary 2 to New York. We got booked up with our travel agent LAH Travel in our village, and set off, well, that was when I realised the perfect travelling companion is myself, as I found I had despite 50 years of friendship my friendship was being questioned. My friend Mary had booked separately but had asked to be put on our table, she was also awaiting surgery and needed a bit of consideration, however you can meet awkward people on trips but to actually have one of them as you're travelling companion can be a bit daunting. However, pin a happy smile on and enjoy what you can. Fortunately there was a delightful American couple at the next table who took to sitting with me in the morning while I awaited my two companions who were not morning people. On the ship I found that when I was with a larger company everyone was very friendly but noticed that when it was just the three of us Mary was sociable but Celia, if I wasn't there was ignoring Mary, this was even more evident as Celia left the dinner table every evening and went to our room, not a happy situation, but not of my doing. We did the theatre shows and on one occasion I particularly wanted to hear Commodore Warwick so suggested we go to his talk. Well Celia and I went as Mary had not appeared, and I was so embarrassed when Celia got up after ten minutes and walked out. Oh dearie me, Rock and hard place.

After that I took to going to the theatre on my own on occasions, or with the lovely American couple Joe and Anne who like me wanted to go to the talks in the mornings. Lynn Truss was so amusing she had us in stitches at both of her talks. Stephen Payne's talk about the designing and building of the ship was terrific and hearing him talking about the old ships fascinating. I enjoyed a chat with him and as I had brought a small clip from old cine film my Dad had taken of the Caronia launch at Clydebank, I asked if he would like a copy, as did charming Captain Oprey when I told him about it, so I trotted off to the photography department and they said I would have to pay to get it copied from my DVD, so my retort was I don't think so the copies are for the Captain and for Mr. Payne who designed the ship. I am delighted to say they obliged so all the recipients got their tiny bit of film. A friend treated us to lunch in Todd English and I was delighted that our waitress spoke Spanish so I got a little chat. This is one of many reasons why I love cruising so much.

The evening entertainments were excellent too, we had a gentleman who showed us how pickpockets work and had people from the audience up on stage, he did give them back their watches belts and ties it was hilarious and educational. The dance shows and the girl's costumes were magnificent. It was a case of fitting everything in, from the dancing lessons in the morning to all the meals, lectures, films. It's a hard life but someone has to do it.

We had got a cab from the dock to the Hotel and that night my niece Catriona and her delightful four boys came for dinner as they could get the train to the Grand Central Station next door to the hotel. John was working as he runs a limousine business. The next morning my niece's husband John had come to get us to take us out for breakfast, so we said to Mary to come but she wasn't ready. John took us to the other side of Central Park to a little café where we had breakfast sitting out on the pavement and then he took us to the museum we thought had the exhibition of the lovely dresses we had read about in the British papers a few weeks earlier, then discovered were at the wrong one, so had a walk through Central Park to the correct one, and once there realised Celia would never manage to walk round. Fortunately there were wheelchairs, so we got one and we went round the exhibition once we got outside again I found a taxi to get us back to the hotel.

I then went to the room where Mary was and said we were back, was asked where we had been, and just said with my nephew. I should have realised at that point I was dealing with two spoiled children not two women of seventy years old. That night we ate in the hotel together but the evening was a short one.

The next problem arose going to the Statue of Liberty, which we got to on a ferry. No sooner were we on board than one wanted to stay down where we had come on and the other wanted to go up on a deck, we went ashore and again one had to sit down so the other two of us went off to see the Statue of Liberty. Shall we say I got to the viewing platform alone as yet again lack of capabilities had prevented my companion from climbing to the observation platform. We had been supposed to go to Ellis Island after that but by the time we had queued to get back on the ferry, which was made easier as my companions' difficulties had been noted and we were told to go to the head of the queue. However by the time we were all back on the boat as the rest of the queue was enormous, and had sailed across to Ellis Island I knew that the two of them couldn't do it and we were running out of time as we had the Theatre that night. We got a cab to the theatre and all seemed well, but I realised rapidly after the show, when all she did was complain about Mary and I singing along to the Jersey Boys, then that she couldn't stand so I had to run up and down the street jumping up and waving in the hope a yellow cab would stop. Eventually one did and we got back to the hotel. We parted company at the hotel and at this point it became evident as back in the room we were sharing, I was told if I ever travelled with Mary again she would not be going. OOPS. That was when I had to go and say to Mary that we would be leaving at a different time and would be in touch later. It was also that we had booked another cruise for the three of us. Next Transatlantic crossing I do will be in one of the single staterooms!

Chapter 15

Seville & Opera

In the meantime Mary and I had booked to go to Seville in the November, as we had booked it ahead to give my husband time to be able to be fully recovered. I had flown to Gatwick the night before as had to be at airport early morning to fly to Seville. Mary was flying from Heathrow to Malaga, as they had changed flights but I had said I had already booked to go to Gatwick so was not prepared to change.

We were staying on a the Guadalquivir River on a River boat called the Belle de Cadix, she was lovely, we arrived about 2pm after being given a lovely coach tour of the city and being able to go and see the Plaza de Espana. The other party flying to Malaga did not arrive until after dinner. The food on board was excellent and the service extremely good.

We also had a trip to Ronda, which was lovely, although the day we were there low cloud was filling the valley and restricted the view of the Roman Viaduct.

The meal at the Parador was splendid and the coach trip most interesting. We were also taken to the Bull Ring which is the original one in Spain, and we saw all the suits of lights and had a tour of the stables. It was an action packed day and such a lot to see.

Mary and I had also opted to go to Granada, which was an extra trip not included, so early in the morning we were boarded onto coaches, and our guide said she would let us have a sleep as so early in the morning, but we would be making a stop for coffee and loos. It was at a roadside café but perfectly adequate for the purpose. When we got back on the coach she then started to tell us about the growing of the olive trees in that area, and also that work had restarted on the railway link from Seville to Granada which had halted due to the financial crisis of 2010. It was worth the long coach ride, as when we got to the Alhambra /Generalife and saw the magnificence of it, with drainage and water supplies.

We had a little free time which enabled a loo break and a coffee, then we were taken on foot down into the town to a Tapas Bar overlooking the city and were given a lovely lunch. The tour guide organised a taxi for some of the less able to get them back to the coach. I walked with a lady who it transpired had been a professional dancer and had been in productions I had seen at the old Alhambra theatre in Glasgow, how strange to find that out on a trip to the Alhambra in Granada.

This view let us see how vast the city of Granada is, we also got a short stop down in the city to have a quick tour for those of us able to walk fast, which was very interesting, and let us see the types of architecture. The ride back was into the evening and we saw a beautiful sunset. Back on the boat and freshen up for dinner, the arrangement was open eating and you just sat at any table, although we had stuck to one near the entrance for convenience as Mary was using a crutch. We had different dining companions, and met some very interesting people. Some afternoons were taken up with talks by Humphrey Burton who in collaboration with the London Festival Opera, and the travel company which arranges these trips.

One evening we were all taken for a formal dinner at **the** King Alphonso Hotel which is magnificent, and the Festival Opera gave a performance in costume before the gala dinner, of pieces from Carmen and Don Giovanni.

Another evening on the boat we had a group come on board to dance flamenco and sing, they were a traditional gypsy group and it was a spell binding performance, it was a wonder the rivets on the boat didn't loosen with the vibration of the male dancers heels.

One day after being on a tour in the city, we were given a little free time and I took the opportunity to go back to a shop selling genuine flamenco dresses as I wanted to get one for my grand- daughters, working on the theory that the elder would wear it first and it could be altered as the seam allowances were terrific. I also bought a touristy one for the younger grand-daughter. What thrilled me most was the lady in the shop did not speak English and I was able to explain what age and height my grand- daughter was and conduct the whole transaction in Spanish. This paid off as the lady put some extra things in like the little shawl and a flower, so I saved some money. It was expensive but I loved seeing her in the dress at Christmas time. The girls in the opera group were very taken with the dress, as was the rep from the travel company who was with us on board.

Another day, we were at the Palace Libreja, where there are a collection of mosaics and roman artefacts, which had been the collection of a lady. She changed the layout of the house to accommodate these wonderful mosaics and the work must have been painstaking to rebuild them, we also could only have a few people upstairs at any one time due to the fragility of the property. Some of the mosaics are rising due to the damp. She had got these mosaics from a place further north where Roman remains had been found called Italica. I would recommend a visit to this house if you have any interest in Roman mosaics. The tiles on the walls of this house are also rescued from various places, and lovingly put together.

There was a most magnificent staircase she had purchased from another house which was being demolished and had installed in her house. We were not allowed to photograph upstairs.

We were given the option of making our own way back to the River. I took that option and had a wander round El Cortes Ingles, then making my way back got a little unsure if heading the correct route, I saw a group of small children with teachers and asked them in Spanish they could direct me, they said no they were just visiting the city, so with that I saw a policeman so approached him and in my best Spanish asked if he could help me and give me directions, I was delighted that not only did he understand me I understood the directions he gave me, and I had a lovely walk back to the boat.

The next day we had a walking tour along into Seville and across to Triana the other side of the river with a visit to a café and shopping area where there were all sorts of stalls selling olives, and snack type foods, tapas, a cakes, we sat out in the sun with our coffees and snacks. Then we continued over the bridge and walked down the other side of the river. We saw a group of schoolchildren practising their Christmas songs at the side of the River, and this was a Sunday. That was bringing the holiday to an end.

Chapter 16

Totally Transfixing Three Queens at Liverpool
on Queen Mary 2

Cunard's 175th Anniversary

Upon embarking at Southampton, as soon as stepping aboard, I felt I had come home. Having done the 10th anniversary crossing on this lovely lady last year to New York I was sure I would not get lost … wrong! However the benefit of this is the extra walking you do it offsets the wonderful variety of food on offer, which of course has to be accompanied by a refreshment of some kind. Captain Wells was again the man in charge, and as many of us had brought mementos of Cunard's history he was always interested in seeing them. I had some from the original Queen Mary which had been my Dad's.

First things first, proceed to your state-room; we don't have humble cabins anymore, all are extremely comfortable. Oh joy, awaiting me a welcome bottle of sparkling wine, fortunately I travel with a champagne cork so I can save and savour it. Unpacking and hanging up, and then time for lunch. Now I know where Kings Court is, of course I do, well I did last year! Fifteen minutes later I have located it and found a space with another solo lady traveller, so tuck in and realise this lady looks familiar, turns out we met a year ago in much the same place on the 10th Anniversary crossing. Lunch over it is time to consider getting the safety training done, so trot back to deck ten and forward to collect necessary life-jacket, and proceed to muster point for the instruction.

At this point we are now getting nearer the time for our departure, so obviously, the place to be is aft and out on deck, once there have the pleasure of meeting one of the waiters Edguardo, who said hello nice to see you again, and he remembers I speak some Spanish. I met him on the 10th Anniversary crossing last year. There were quite a few waiters and bar waiters I remembered from last year Joan pronounced Jo- an and his wife who also works on board, the three of them are from Argentina and encouraged my attempts at Spanish. Sail-away was brilliant as always, and then it was time to get tidied up and off for first sitting dinner. Having been escorted to my table I was delighted with my table companions, Brenda and Kay, and another lady and our one gentleman Alfred seemed to be happy to have four ladies to chat to. The fourth lady kept referring to her late husbands, as husband number one and husband number two we felt perhaps she was on the lookout for the next one! The sixth person remained a mystery as the chair remained empty. Indeed it remained empty for the whole voyage, but we had a name of a lady, and due to the fact there were a lot of Japanese people on board wondered if she was one of them and perhaps didn't speak English. We will never know! However, our waiters and sommelier were excellent and realised pretty soon, that madam loves fish and cheese, can't eat cream or ice-cream, and apart from that is very happy to listen to recommendations.

The next day at breakfast in Britannia restaurant, I was placed at a table with a spare seat, a good way to meet more people! Two ladies at the table said they had only sailed with P & O before so I said I had not sailed with P & O but my sister in law and brother in law do regularly and they very much enjoy it. I go with Cunard because it suits me, and have no intention of going with any other line.

The variety of entertainment offered was as usual with my beloved Cunard top notch and the biggest problem is trying to fit it all in. Caroline Aston's first talk was on in the theatre, but full house standing room only. I watched it later on TV in my room. However at that point met two ladies I had previously met eleven years ago and had not seen since, so we went and had coffee and a chat.

First port Cobh, or as Captain Wells said in his address at the cocktail party Ringaskiddy, then coaches into Cork where a most enjoyable walking tour was my choice, I loved the history and we had free time at the English Market to look round and get a coffee and cake, as though we never saw cake on a daily basis at present! The tour guides had told us about the Queen's visit to Cork and the market and how the owner of one of the fish stalls had entertained Her Majesty and has written a book about it. It was a fabulous market and the foodstuffs were very tempting, but we didn't need to buy food.

The tour guides we had on our coach were hilarious and one also called Eleanor and I had a great banter or craic. The other lady sang to us in Gaelic and tried to teach us some words, ending up with the whole coachload singing the Wild Rover as we were approaching the dockside. On leaving the coach each and everyone got a hug from both these exceptionally warm-hearted Irish ladies.

Next port Dublin via Dun Laoghaire, and a tender port. Well that is dependent on the weather improving, so as this was all looking extremely doubtful, as one trip had to be cancelled due to shortage of time, an alternative programme for the rest of the day was quickly drawn up which included a talk by Dr. Stephen Payne about

Lusitania and Mauretania, which was fabulous, loved it. Also due to this Caroline Aston did an extra one, up to and including our present Royal family, which was hilarious. What talented speakers they are.

However late morning it was decided the weather had subsided enough to enable the tenders to be put out, and off we sailed for land.

I was meeting my friend's daughter in law for lunch who was coming out from Dublin to meet me, thank goodness, as this particular Brain of Britain had left her money in the safe in her room, and realised half-way across the expanse of sea. However, Emma kindly paid and took me to a lovely restaurant beside the marina. While waiting for her had a good look around the town and enjoyed looking out to see Queen Mary 2 anchored out in the Bay,

I met a team of the ship's photographers and one of them told me he had also forgotten his money, but he had his colleagues with him. I also met a couple who had brought Pounds instead of Euros, so felt slightly less stupid!

The theatre shows were excellent, and the comedians extremely funny and I thoroughly enjoyed the shows. The entertainment was tremendous.

By now I had met a couple Ed and Maggie, previously encountered as table companions on Queen Elizabeth's Maiden Baltic voyage when it was their first Cunard trip, so obviously they had enjoyed that and here we were again. This tied in with Captain Wells' remark about us being Cunarders.

Next port in the South West of Scotland my home territory and a long held dream about to come true, as I am fortunate to stay in a house with an unbroken view of Ailsa Craig, and the Isle of Arran, which means I watch all the ships coming up and down, and had promised myself many years ago that one day I would go past my house on a liner. Well as we know there is only one, so that morning I was up and out on deck at 4.30am, seem to have missed Ailsa Craig, but received a phone call from my husband to say I just saw you sail past on your "boat" I gave him boat when I got back home! I saw the pilot get on and enjoyed watching the coast of North Ayrshire become Inverclyde until we docked at Greenock. On the quayside there was a pipe-band playing to welcome us in, and we were alongside by 7.00am. I was sorry for my fellow passengers that it was so bitterly cold, and even I found it freezing. However after meeting up with friends Anne and her son Robert, who had come to see the ship from the shore and having coffee, they went home and I went to meet my friend Kathryn for lunch. I made sure I had money as it was her daughter in law Emma who had saved me from myself in Eire. After she left to go home I came back on board to heat up. The entertainment before we left was tremendous and as a biased Scotswomen I was very proud of the quality of the performance, especially the piping, I am married to a piper, and a good one! That coupled with the pipe band on the dockside and the fireworks later, was quite emotional, especially as our lovely wee "Waverley" was in attendance, the last ocean going paddle-steamer in the world, together with the only liner in the world. There is also now a new tartan Cunard on the Clyde commissioned by Peel Ports in celebration of the 175th anniversary, and bonny it is too.

That night the fireworks were stupendous, and you could see the nose to tail traffic right down the coast road, Kathryn with whom I had lunch sent me photos by phone and said wave! I obliged.

It transpires as I found out after returning home, that a lot of people right down the coast had a very late night, as they stayed up to see our return down the Clyde from Greenock, one elderly gentleman I know who lives at Portencross, a hamlet beside West Kilbride, Ayrshire and across from Great Cumbrae was in his bed and just dropping off to sleep when his house shook and he was awakened by the horn of Queen Mary 2, he said it sounded like the original Clyde built one, which he knows is on QM2! That was just after the pilot had got off, which I was watching from the deck. Amazing to see how they leave a giant to get onto a little pilot boat!

At this point I thought if that's what we get at Greenock, what we get at Liverpool is going to be truly amazing. Is there a word greater than amazing, as what was to follow is hard to describe adequately.

Next on the list was Oban, which like many Captain Wells pronounced Obaan, instead of our clipped Obn. However, more rain still cold and this time I remembered the purse but forgot the bank card. However Royal Bank of Scotland despite its flaws came up trumps as I had a copy of my passport with me and was able to lay my paws on some cash which I immediately spent at the shoe shop further along, as my tootsies were finding the dressy shoes I had brought a tad on the tight side. Then

I went back to the ship as I know Oban well, and fancied being on the ship more.

We then had a sea day from Oban down to Liverpool for the start of the big celebration. I was in the company of some Japanese ladies who were busy writing down words for me as they had decided to teach me some Japanese words. One of the ladies had quite good English and some of the others only a little and one older lady none at all, so at least trying to say these words was being very well received.

Liverpool what a beautiful sight coming to the Liver Building, the Cunard Building, The Port Authority "The Three Graces", the welcome from Liverpool was amazing, I got ashore as desperate to see the Maritime Museum and this did not disappoint what fabulous exhibitions, the street entertainments were varied and entertaining, and all the buzz on the river of the little boats and the dazzle ferry, all adding to the atmosphere.

That evening, having had yet another beautiful special dinner, we gathered on deck for the light show on the buildings and more wonderful fireworks, Champagne was available on deck so I gave in gracefully and got some. Once that was over, I adjourned to Sir Samuels, where sense told me that as bubbles followed by wine are not a good idea I would just stick to champagne. I had been hoping to meet a friend, but due to his official capacity this did not prove possible. It was during this evening that the dignitaries from Liverpool had been aboard and next day Captain Wells told us Cunard had been given the Freedom of Liverpool. To be able to say I was aboard when this honour was given was a lovely feeling.

Next morning, we left to wonderful music, Nessun Dorma, Rule Britannia, Land of Hope and Glory, even though the recording of the Leaving of Liverpool stuck and became quite amusing, it was nonetheless very emotional. We then sailed off to meet our sister ships, and still had the Beatles Experience on board and playing on deck for us, great fun, when the other two ships hove into view it was seeing a promise come true they sailed past us and we turned and came back in with them, before the most wonderful river dance of three great big ships was performed, at this point the atmosphere aboard could only be described as electric. Waving from ship to ship, cheers, and so on, photos being taken from all angles, even the crew where possible coming out to see, to my delight I got a photo taken with two, as without these guys we would go nowhere! I was in excellent company with a couple I had met previously on the 10th anniversary transatlantic who are hilarious, and they were having a ball, I do hope I meet them again.

Then we sailed off down the Mersey and out to sea, and afternoon tea.

Afternoon tea was magnificent with the 175 in icing and the Ice Sculptures of the Ship and Singapore's Merlion, the cakes were amazing, chocolate cups filled with mousse and a square of white chocolate with the 175 logo on. So many to choose from, sponge, chocolate, lemon, and also the sandwiches and scones........... not forgetting the lovely cups of tea!

More tea Madam, don't mind if I do................love this life.

Our final port before returning to Southampton was Guernsey and last tender port, by which time Captain Wells thought we should be experts, getting onto on and off them.

Once on Guernsey I with another 89 people took a tiny ferry to Sark. When you get off the ferry you climb steps up onto the quayside depending on how high the tide is, then you walk through a short tunnel and at the other end there is a tractor with a bus type open sided trailer which is called the toast-rack, as that is exactly if put on its side what it looks like. The other side is filled in, and this takes you up the hill into the village. Once in the village you can get a carriage ride for £10 which takes you over a lot of the island and they stop to let you walk down a field where there is a view to the other Channel Islands.

We had a very pleasant time ashore with time to have a wander, and a carriage ride which let us get to viewpoints where we could see France, Alderney, and Jersey, learn a bit about the island which now only has a population of 450. Some of the leaflets we saw have a larger number shown for population but the man whose Carriage we were on said that was a number of years ago, as the young people have to leave and don't always come back. I spent the day with the lady I had met at lunch the first day as she was also on her own.

We had lunch at a little tearoom and paying was interesting as we could pay in Euros or Sterling but got Guernsey money in change. Once back on Guernsey from the little ferry, we were transported back to the ship on the bigger tourist boat which was bringing back the shore crew and the coffee pots, so that was really easy to get on and off. What a beautiful island and made me aware of how vulnerable they were, especially when it was pointed out that a windmill had been used by the Germans as a lookout post.

Lovely scenery and welcoming people, who said they are so dependent on tourists visiting for their livelihood; they are self- sufficient in dairy produce and have their own electricity generating station, but of course everything else has to come by sea.

After returning to the ship, we had a slightly later dinner, most of us exchanged addresses, went to check we had our cases packed and out, and then Alfred, who was excellent company to us ladies, asked me to join him for a chat and drink in the Chart Room, I then went to the Queens Room, to thank the Gentlemen Hosts for their company, and dancing with me.

Next morning early final breakfast, some more farewells and sadly time to leave the ship to go to the airport to return to Glasgow.

Chapter 17

After the rain Queen Victoria and Spain!

After an awful summer of rain I decided to book another cruise so opted for Queen Victoria to Spain and Morocco in November 2015

Fast forward now to November and I flew to Southampton to join the Queen Victoria, as I had not yet sailed on her. I had gone early as do not like flying the same day as the ship sails. I had decided to treat myself to a dinner and show at the Mayflower theatre. The tickets had been posted to me so all I had to do was to remember to take them with me.

I arrived at Southampton airport and my pre-booked taxi took me to the Ibis only snag I had booked the Ibis Budget by mistake. I checked in and when I went to the room discovered it had a toilet, and a shower, but the basin was in the bedroom, and there was no tea or coffee making facility, it looked like a prison cell from a television show, apart from the double bed. I went back downstairs and across to the Ibis where I had stayed previously and asked if they had a room. Thank goodness they did, and gave me a decent price for the two nights, and when I said what it had made me think of, they said that they call it the Prison. I then went back to the budget hotel and got my cases and handed back the key card. I had to forfeit the charge for that night but it was a small price to pay to get a decent room. I was able to claim back the second night the next day from Booking.com who was helpful.

The lady at the Ibis said that the Budget hotel had previously been called Etap, which is why I didn't realise I was booking the wrong one. I went next door to the Novotel and got a nice dinner, then as it was Sunday night went to my room and watched the Strictly results show, and the Antique Road Show before going to bed.

After breakfast the next morning I got directions to the West Quay shopping mall, and had a lovely wander in and out of the shops for a good part of the morning, resisting buying anything as the cases were packed. I went back to the hotel and had a light snack, then put the feet up and read for a couple of hours, before getting ready to go to the theatre for my meal and the show.

At the theatre I and some other ladies were taken up to the lovely restaurant, and I was introduced to my waiters, one from Cadiz and one from Valencia, oh joy! I took the chance of practising my Spanish. We were then taken through to the theatre and the show which was "The Full Monty". It was hilarious and the bulk of the audience were of course women.

I had booked a taxi to pick me up, and as I was waiting for it two ladies offered to take me back to the hotel, which I thanked them for but my taxi was there.

I had the room till mid-day but cleared out about eleven the next morning, and waited downstairs, as I had a taxi booked to take me to the dock. Check in went smoothly as I now qualified for priority check in as a platinum level Cunarder. I got to my inside cabin which is one of the new singles, and it was very roomy, with lots of drawer space. As my bags didn't arrive for quite a while I entertained myself by opening a bottle of champagne which had been sent as a gift. My champagne cork was in my case so I put the napkin over the top to save the bubbles, must make a note to put in hand luggage next time. I wrote a couple of notes and left one on the next cabin for my friend who was joining me on this one, despite cancelling May's trip. Also I had heard from Brenda I had met on QM2 on the same table in May that she was coming on this one, so had her cabin number and popped up to leave a note for her

Eventually the cases arrived, and I got unpacked quite quickly as with all that drawer space I had no problem where to put stuff.

My friend Mary arrived and was a bit late, as she had got a taxi to bring her from London as she was concerned about getting to the coach transfer in time. However, we agreed we would go along for dinner together as had arranged to be on same table.

We got to our table and met a couple and two other ladies, who were on it, and after finishing our meal, Mary and I left and went to find a corner to sit and chat, we were not exactly enchanted with the two other women who had virtually ignored the couple and ourselves. My friend and I went to the show as Benjamin Makisi was in the Welcome Aboard show, and she thought he was marvellous too.

I had gone down to the press office to make sure that our Cunard Critic forum gathering had been put into the daily programme, and met Anne in her office. It was all set up.

A group of us through the internet had arranged to meet at 11 o'clock in the Commodore Club for Champagne and other drinks; we had quite a good turn out and met most of the people we had been in touch with. While we were meeting, Brenda who had been on my table in May came in to the Commodore Club, so we asked her to come and join us then Mary eventually appeared as well. After that gathering the three of us had a discussion to the effect we went to see the Maître D' to say we would like to be seated together. He managed to put us upstairs in Club Balcony on a table for three, it was perfect. Brenda had been at the other side of the restaurant from us and was not too enamoured of the company she had been put with either.

That evening in the theatre the comedian Allan Stewart was performing and he was excellent, I had seen him previously at a friends' party when he was the cabaret, and again on Queen Elizabeth on the Baltic Cruise. He is an excellent entertainer. The three of us thoroughly enjoyed the show.

Earlier after dinner Michael had come and whispered to us that he had arranged for them to renew their vows, but Angie didn't yet know, so a couple of days later when he told her, she said to us and you all knew before me, we just smiled and said so we did. They very kindly invited us to the ceremony but only Brenda went as I had booked a trip to Cordoba that day, Sunday 8th their anniversary.

The shows were excellent, Ben Makisi the Maori opera singer with the most glorious voice. The ships dancers and singers were brilliant and altogether we had most nights at the show before Brenda would have a shot on the slot machines, which proved profitable for her, while I liked to go to dancing and quite often Michael and Angie joined me. Mary had taken to excusing herself. Beginning to feel like history repeating but we will reserve judgement! Our first port after two sea days' was La Corunna, and I had booked a trip to Santiago de Compostela, as know people who had walked the Camino. It was a very interesting but extremely wet day, so we got soaked, and my first purchase was an umbrella as I had left mine on the ship. It was not the best of umbrellas, but helped. It was very interesting seeing inside the Cathedral, and also in the church where the nuns are in a closed order, as we were quietly looking round with our guide speaking very quietly a hidden hand started to play the organ and the music was beautiful. We then went to a very old building for coffee and cake, and this was previously a monastery, the gates were still there, very reminiscent of a scene from the "Sound of Music" film. We also saw a brass shell in one of the little street showing the Pilgrim Way.

We saw a group known as Tuna who are students and form groups playing music, they wear black capes but have colourful ribbons on the back; it was hard to photograph in the rain.

On the way back to the coach there was a deluge which just ran off the umbrella and we all had wet legs.

Once back on the ship it was good to get dry clothes on, and meet up at dinner and compare notes. Even the trip to La Corunna got rained on but not to the extent we had seemingly! I heard that umbrellas had been getting handed out! Must have been after we left as rain hadn't got started when we left! That evening we went to see the show in the Theatre which was lovely, the singers and dancers are top rate.

The next day I had booked a hot stone massage at the Spa, and had originally booked for mid-day however the spa staff had suggested I come after breakfast, I was so glad it had been changed as the benefits of that I am sure warded off a chill from the soaking the day before as I had been sore and stiff when I got up. A treat I will repeat.

The next day was a sea day we had all day to do whatever took our fancy. I had by this time handed a book about the 175 years history to the purser's office along with first day covers with the request that the Commodore sign them for me. I had also included some from a friend who collects them. I had promised to get him a model of the ship and get it signed. That evening was the Black & White Ball preceded by the welcome Cocktail Party in the Queen's Room. The social hostess asked everyone their name as they came in and announced them before they greet the Commodore. I gave my name at which point Sally promptly announced me as a Mr and Mrs, I turned to her and said no no just

Mrs. Mr. isn't here he is at home. She said sorry I burst out laughing as did others around and Commodore Rynd had a big smile on his face. I then explained I was the cause of the pile of stuff in his office and he asked "what did I want done with them?", so I said please sign them. We had a great night in the Ballroom, and I had already re-met Wilfried and Ilona the professional dance teachers, I had previously met two years earlier on the 10th anniversary crossing. I was amazed they remembered me. Later that night a young woman came up and said "Eleanor?" I said yes, it was Cat the assistant social hostess also from that trip. This is why Cunard are special.

Our next port was Cadiz and I had booked a walking tour, which started from the ship and took us right up into the town, and through narrow streets, it was fascinating, and the sun was shining although there was a bit of a wind blowing, but it was lovely. The tour started at a marvellous statue which commemorates the forming of the Constitution in 1812. Again this was a lot of information to take in but the guide was excellent. We came to a house in one of the street with brass hands for door knockers.

This was the home of a famous Spanish composer, Don Manuel de Falla Mateu. She made a joke about her learning English and discovering rapidly that when she used the plural of knocker, any English speaking groups would burst out laughing. Fortunately someone had the good grace to explain to the girl, and now she is very careful how she describes the hands on the door!

We had a stop in a square for coffee, and then had free time. I had brought a red dress with me but didn't like the thin stole with it so was looking for something more to cover my shoulders. Lady luck was on my side, as I wandered down past shops, including C & A much to the amusement of many of us Brits, as no longer available in the UK, I found a shop with the sign in the window "Liquidación", now even if you don't speak Spanish that is self- explanatory. I was in there like a shot as in the window they had red satin bolero style jackets for 10

Euros. I asked in Spanish if I could try them on but had to be red. I got a beauty, and when I got back to the ship was delighted it was a perfect match; I had been prepared to have a near match! I hadn't thought to take the dress with me as I was travelling light while doing walking tours!

I met up with a lovely couple from St. Andrews on the east coast of Scotland so we were going about together and she was wanting help with buying a handbag, she asked how do say thank you so I was telling her the words to use. She got her bargain, and then when I told her about the shop I had been in, we did a quick dash back to see if she could get anything. They didn't have what she was looking for.

Some people had gone into a building which had previously been the Post Office and was now a food market; their reports were that it was amazing, so next time I get to Cadiz will need to investigate that. We had the options of walking the whole way back to the ship or leaving the group part way back, I opted for the whole way back as was feeling I wanted to get rid of my bag and purchases, including a fridge magnet, for a souvenir to keep for myself.

The plaza we walked down to return to the ship, and just before we got to the ship there was a lovely fountain with fishes sculpted on it and was just across the road from the ship.

Once back on board I met Angie who said to go to the Winter Garden to join them so I got my things back in my room and did just that. Sitting in the sun but not in it directly was lovely.

I then said I would whizz up to the spa for a dip, little did I realise the surprise I would get, I got into my swimsuit and went into the pool area, saw an oriental man wrapped in a towel at the loungers and continued into the pool, Well.... At the side of the pool are two showers to use before and after being in the pool clothed, and as I turned round once in the pool, there was, fortunately with his back to me, an oriental gent without a stitch on! Oh dear not happening I tiptoed out the pool got my bathrobe and flip flops went to the door which opens automatically, and fortunately the girl who had given me my massage was passing, so I said I had a problem as there was a naked man in the shower at the poolside! She said she would get the manager who went and spoke to the man who it transpired did not speak English, but he thought had made him understand. Ok… I went back, but no he didn't understand, as still not left the shower, so absented myself and said problem not solved. It transpired the gent was used to male only spa's in Japan and had not realised on a ship it was mixed, just a slight culture difference! The Japanese words from the ladies I met in May on QM2 were not the ones I needed in this instance!

At a later point when speaking to the Commodore and other officers, I related this experience and said I had gone to the theatre in Southampton the night before joining the ship I really had not needed that as I had seen "The Full Monty". They had a laugh at that! Later I went and had afternoon tea with crust less sandwiches and lovely cakes. I always find it amusing that they serve the tea, the sandwiches, and then the cakes, with the scones with cream and jam last. I have to forego the cream, but the rest is no problem. I had also become impressed with the fact that each night at dinner, I was presented with the menu for the next day, so I could choose and discuss any dish, to avoid an allergy. They have one chef who does the special meals, in the kitchen, which I had verified when I did the behind the scenes tour.

The show that night was Dance Passion and was covering all types of dance and was quite spectacular, afterwards it was time to adjourn to the Queen's Ballroom for some more dancing, and socialising with Angie Michael and Brenda.

Next day after docking at Malaga, I was on a trip to Cordoba, chosen as had been able to see Granada the previous year, and been told Cordoba was as spectacular in a different way. We left at 10.30 for our two hour drive, and half way stopped for a comfort break and coffee if desired. I was sitting with a lady from Australia who was keen on photography, and like me was finding the tour guide's constant commentary difficult to take in as it was truly non- stop, too much information. She was a delightful young woman obviously good at her job, but to keep that up for two hours, then into the city and round the city. I was glad when we went for lunch. It was in a delightful little restaurant, and we were given a local tomato soup with chopped egg in it, called "Salmorejo cordobes" we were all given a card with the recipe on the back. Only snag about reproducing this in the UK would be the "pan de Telera" obviously a local bread. The next course a ham dish, which some people didn't want or didn't eat pork so chicken was got for them. There was wine and coffee with it and was in lovely surroundings. There was a picture of a horse and dog nuzzling each other which was very appealing.

On the way to the Mosque we went through an artisan area where quite clearly in Spanish it said do not photograph on the wall of a silver studio, well one woman, despite me saying, did just that. Shortly afterwards this irate silversmith came and shouted that she wanted the photos deleted. I said to the woman in question, you better do that, but she said she would when she was ready. She did say later she had, but it was quite embarrassing for the group and especially for the guide.

We then went to the Mosque which was very interesting and at this point I could take in the information from the guide, who had provided us with radio earphones so we could follow what she was saying.

Stunning is the word which came to mind, I would say more so than Granada. It was just so much information to take in, which is where having a book to read later is useful.

That was the day Angie and Michael were renewing their vows, and as I didn't get back till 7.00pm I was unable to be with them for this occasion, as I had booked the trip. He had done it as a surprise for Angie, had just told her to bring her dress as she could wear it as an evening dress. This was their seventh anniversary but as in the last two years life had been very difficult due to severe health problems this was to celebrate Angie being much better.

Michael said "don't rush go and get something to eat", so I got showered and changed and grabbed some food at the Lido and went and joined them in the Commodore Club. They were wearing the outfits from their wedding seven years earlier and the ship's florist had done flowers in the colours Angie had then, also a lovely rich fruit cake had been made also. It was delicious. This was the "Cunard Critic" who had come to celebrate with Angie and Michael. Then we had the VIP visitors too.

Commodore Rynd and James Cusick, Hotel Manager, came to join us for a while, and I was glad to be able to explain to James why I had to decline his invitation to dinner the next night, as Michael, Angie and I were going to the Verandah for our dinner.

We stayed there all evening until time to go to bed. Brenda had been at the ceremony and came and joined us, as did one of the singers from the Cunard singers, and her parents who were on board too. Another couple we had met through the Cunard forum came too, Joan and Jim from the USA and a couple of Aussie's who were on honeymoon, altogether we had a great party, with people coming and going.

The next day it was the port of Tangiers, and my trip was to Tetuan in the Rif Mountains, it was quite a lengthy journey but our guide an elderly Moroccan gentleman made it clear that Morocco does not want to be involved in all the troubles around, he said we all have the same God by different names, and from the reports from the other coaches on the other tours all the guides were saying the same. As we were driving out of Tangiers, I saw a man bringing his herd of goats down a side street. It is a city of contrast as there are the big international hotels near the centre and where the ships can be seen docked, and then as you go out into the country he explained that some buildings were the former border controls when operated by the French. French is the language in most of Morocco, but in Tetuan they still speak Spanish, which suited me fine. We saw a farmer ploughing with a tractor on his small farm, as they had a little rain the week before and were hoping for more the coming week, so were preparing to plant wheat. Further along the road was another farmer ploughing with mules!

There was a lot of open land with the fields sometimes with goats grazing while we were on the coach going to Tetuan.

Passing through villages there were street markets with the vegetables displayed on the pavements, also the terracotta tagines.

There women in their national dress at some of these street markets, and very colourful they were sitting beside their vegetables for sale. Arriving at Tetuan it struck me how many cars there were coming into the city, when we had been passing a truly rural landscape being farmed traditionally.

Once we got to Tetuan, we also had a local guide who stressed we must stay together, and we had a guard at each side, at one point in the Medina I stopped to look at some sort of seeds like sunflower or similar, and he came back and said what do you want to know, so after he told me the name of the seed, he said come lady come, so I did as I was told and re-joined the group.

Our guide was a lovely Moroccan man dressed traditionally in his djellaba, he explained that the ladies wear Kaftans, and do not have a hood. He was joking he sometimes put his lunch in his hood. He took us to see the Mosque built in the 15th century.   There was another doorway around the same part of the Medina which was very colourfully painted with a date inscribed above it.

We ended up in a market square where a man was selling a green powder, our guide kidded us it was hashish; he then confessed it was henna for hair colour. A lady at a stall nearby dressed one of us in the national dress, she looked the part.

We were then taken to a house which was signposted as the Palace Bouhal salon where we were given Mint tea and a biscuit, very much like a melting moment biscuit. We were also told to use the necessaries, which is how they refer to toilets as there are no public toilets on the way back to the coach. They told us how they make the mint tea, and we had been given fresh mint while walking through the Medina to the Salon. It was also interesting that the tiles on the walls explaining what the buildings are were in different languages, as well as Arabic these signs were in Spanish and English.

We had the baker shop pointed out to us and the trays with the bread being left to rise. A little further on we found another baker's where our local guide asked if he could have six loaves to share among us so we could taste the hot bread. It was delicious. These little bakers are tiny and there are quite a number of them. The bread also gets sold on stalls along with other things like cartons of juice.

After that we were given the chance to visit an artisan craft place, the women worked upstairs, but as the stairs were steep I opted to stay downstairs, and found a gorgeous Kaftan. The man wanted 90 euros, so I said I only had 25 euros he then said 50 euros so I repeated only had 25 euros, he agreed to the 25 euros if I gave him 3 euros for coffee, I only had four so gave him that, I got the kaftan which is beautifully hand finished, and was told later it was a real bargain.

I had already bought a handbag for 10 euros while we were going through the Medina, and we were told only to hand over the money with the guard with us. When we got outside again, there was the man now offering me a Tagine, I declined, a kaftan is manageable in a suitcase a tagine I doubt if it would get there in one piece. We made our way back to the coaches. On the way back to Tangier, I was watching from the coach as I had seen interesting things on the way to Tetuan, and as we passed the reservoir it just looked like a sandy area with what we would refer to as a large puddle. The level of this had been referred to on the way into Tetuan.

I saw a group of women knocking the olives off the trees onto mats as we drove past. Our guide told us that the olives are picked in October for green olives, November for red olives and December for black olives.

That night we had the Royal Ascot Ball, so as I had brought a hat with me, I was going to wear it, other ladies had brought hats too and some were stunning. The prize went to a lady who had made herself a topper with 175 on it and very good it was too. I sat with Angie and Michael and we had a lovely evening. Michael even escorted me round the floor for the hat parade.

The next day was yet another port this time Lisbon, and as I had been there previously on more than one occasion I had opted for a trip to a village called Obidos.

This is a medieval village with cobbled narrow streets and very picturesque, there were other Cunard passengers visiting too from Queen Elizabeth which was in port with us, and a football match had been arranged between the two ships.

We were back before the footballers and we saw them arriving back and found out "our" team from Queen Victoria had won 9-0, Queen Elizabeth was just starting her voyage having come from Southampton to Lisbon and was going on to the Canary Islands. The visit to Obidos was very good it is a charming medieval little town, still with its narrow streets, unspoiled, with a castle. While on the coach the guide was explaining that there are towns being developed as commuter towns for Lisbon, and that the rail links are very important.

Sail away from Lisbon was lovely as the sun was getting lower and there up ahead was Queen Elizabeth leaving after her first port of her latest voyage. That night was informal so I decided to wear the Kaftan, which was well received by all who saw it and said "did you get that in Tangiers?" Answer, "No in Tetuan" and it was a most comfortable garment to wear, definitely part of my now organised cruise wardrobe.

We then had two sea days back to Southampton, including another cocktail party. While at the cocktail party Cat the social hostess came up and said did you get my letter? I said no, so she told me I had the winning bid for the Chart of the Voyage and could collect it from the purser's office. The following morning I collected it and found it was in a huge cardboard tube, so as returning by plane from Southampton, asked if it could be posted to me, and it was.

The next day was Remembrance Day 11th November, there was a service of remembrance in the theatre which was full with standing room only. They relayed the service to the Golden Lion Pub as an overflow. It was somehow more moving being on a ship as the movement of the ship was poignant. There were several passengers wearing their medals as well as some of the shipboard personnel.

Later that same day I did the behind the scenes tour, we started with the stage and were shown several lighting effects, and behind the stage and in the dressing rooms, the deck where the chains and anchors are sent to the deep, and how the ship is secured when docked, seeing where all the garbage disposal is done, the hi tech controls for the engines, and the storage of the vast amounts of food which we consume. We had a visit to the baker and shown how all the different breads are prepared, and then in the kitchens with the head chef we were given lovely little cakes and a drink of juice or coffee, before going and seeing where our meals are prepared. The icing on the cake so to speak was the visit to the bridge, and seeing how the ship is steered nowadays. Lastly we had photographs taken sitting in the Commodores chair with him beside us and were given a small gift as a memento.

As our cruise was drawing to an end, Angie and Michael spent a lot of time with me and it transpired Michael and Angie had been having fun with their collection of Cunard Bears, they were taking photos of the Teddies on Tour and those Teddies were getting everywhere. They were giving a lot of people on board entertainment.

On our last morning on board we had another Cunard Critic meeting and tried out more of the cocktail menu. As it was coffee time I had a coffee based one which was very good. Next move? Book another Cunard cruise! I have! Guaranteed good company and great fun!

These stories are from some of my more memorable trips and I hope you have enjoyed reading about them.

18905931R00150

Printed in Great Britain
by Amazon